P9-DTT-667

Who Kidnapped
Excellence?

Who Kidnapped Excellence?

What Stops Us From Giving and Being Our Best

HARRY PAUL

JOHN BRITT

ED JENT

BK

Berrett–Koehler Publishers, Inc.
San Francisco
a BK Business book

Berrett-Koehler Publishers, Inc.
235 Montgomery Street, Suite 650
San Francisco, CA 94104-2916
Tel: (415) 288-0260   Fax: (415) 362-2512   www.bkconnection.com

Ordering Information

Quantity sales. Special discounts are available on quantity purchases by corporations, associations, and others. For details, contact the "Special Sales Department" at the Berrett-Koehler address above.

Individual sales. Berrett-Koehler publications are available through most bookstores. They can also be ordered directly from Berrett-Koehler: Tel: (800) 929-2929; Fax: (802) 864-7626; www.bkconnection.com.

Orders for college textbook/course adoption use. Please contact Berrett-Koehler: Tel: (800) 929-2929; Fax: (802) 864-7626.

Orders by U.S. trade bookstores and wholesalers. Please contact Ingram Publisher Services, Tel: (800) 509-4887; Fax: (800) 838-1149; E-mail: customer.service@ingrampublisherservices.com; or visit www. ingrampublisherservices.com/Ordering for details about electronic ordering.

Printed in the United States of America

Berrett-Koehler books are printed on long-lasting acid-free paper. When it is available, we choose paper that has been manufactured by environmentally responsible processes. These may include using trees grown in sustainable forests, incorporating recycled paper, minimizing chlorine in bleaching, or recycling the energy produced at the paper mill.

Library of Congress Cataloging-in-Publication Data

Paul, Harry, 1950-

Who kidnapped excellence? : what stops us from giving and being our best / Harry Paul, John Britt, Ed Jent. -- First edition.

pages cm

Summary: "In this entertaining parable, bestselling authors Paul and Britt tell how to give and be your best in five critical work dimensions -- passion, competency, flexibility, communication, and ownership -- and foster excellence in your organization" -- Provided by publisher.

Includes bibliographical references and index.

ISBN 978-1-62656-087-1 (hardback)

1. Organizational effectiveness. 2. Work ethic. 3. Employee motivation. 4. Success in business. 5. Success. I. Britt, John, 1962- II. Jent, Ed. III. Title.

HD58.9.P383 2014

658.3'14--dc23   2013031040

First Edition

19 18 17 16 15 14   10 9 8 7 6 5 4 3 2 1

Interior design/art: Laura Lind Design   Editor: Elissa Rabellino
Cover design: Irene Morris Design   Proofreader: Henri Bensussen
Production service: Linda Jupiter Productions

To Jack Paul

My father, he lived life with zest.

—HARRY PAUL

To Freda C. Embry,

My second mother

—JOHN BRITT

To Patricia Jent

My beautiful wife,

who is not only a great encourager

but a source of inspiration.

You are the best!

—ED JENT

CONTENTS

Foreword

I'm a Raving Fan of John Britt and Harry Paul. I was one of the coauthors with John of *Who Killed Change?* and wrote the foreword to *FISH!*, which Harry coauthored. They are two of the most creative people I know.

As you read *Who Kidnapped Excellence?*, you soon find out that John, Harry, and Ed Jent exemplify the concept that one plus one is a lot greater than two. Their creativity will immediately come alive for you in this parable in which Gorman-Scott Inc.'s team of Passion, Competency, Flexibility, Communication, and Ownership must battle Average's team of N. Different, N. Ept, N. Flexibility, Miss Communiction, and Poser to win back their Excellence. You will see why the same battle must be fought not only at your workplace but also at home with your family.

Read *Who Kidnapped Excellence?* Share it with everybody at work and at home, enjoy the story, and be ready to practice what you learn about yourself and how you can continually bring excellence into your life and the organizations to which you belong.

Ed Jent, who has a background in ministry of education, joins John and Harry and adds a distinct flavor to this book. Thanks, John, Harry, and Ed. You're the best.

Ken Blanchard
Coauthor, *The One Minute Manager®* and
Fit at Last: Look and Feel Better Once and for All

Introduction

Who *Kidnapped Excellence? What Stops Us From Giving and Being Our Best* is written for YOU! Whether you are a frontline employee, supervisor, manager, CEO, mother, father, or spouse, this book has a personal message for you. It is intended for people to use both in their organizational roles and in their personal lives.

In *Who Kidnapped Excellence?*, Excellence gets kidnapped at Gorman-Scott Inc. and is replaced by Average, who is a makeup artist. Interestingly, months go by before Leadership recognizes the change. A ransom note left on the conference room table is the impetus that sets Leadership in motion to get their Excellence back. Leadership enlists Excellence's team (Passion, Competency, Flexibility, Communication, and Ownership) in the quest.

But Average is not easily thwarted. He assembles his own team (N. Different, N. Competency, N. Flexibility, Miss Communication, and Poser), who dig in their heels and use all their cunning powers of deception to keep Excellence from returning and to keep Performance falling.

CAST OF CHARACTERS

Excellence	Average
Passion	N. Different
Competency	N. Ept
Flexibility	N. Flexibility
Communication	Miss Communication
Ownership	Poser

As this organizational good-versus-evil confrontation unfolds, Dave, the long-standing deliveryman for Gorman-Scott Inc., comes face-to-face with Average in his personal life. The stories of Dave and the organization intertwine in their common challenges: first, they need to fully recognize the presence of Average, and then they need to return Excellence to her rightful place.

In the "Resources" section, Dave offers practical advice to help others gain and maintain excellence in their personal lives and their work. The last section, "People and Companies Who 'Get It,'" offers insight into people and companies who demonstrate excellence.

Note to the Reader

Most companies talk about excellence on a routine basis. Yet we do so without a common definition. How do we define excellence? When we began this book, we initially identified many qualities of excellence. However, over the course of two and a half years, we whittled the number down to five. This was no easy task. As we examined these qualities, we realized that many of the traits were actually a subset of one of the five core qualities.

Now we believe we have identified those core qualities/ elements of excellence. Additionally, we believe that in this book we have created a common language that more accurately defines and explains the concept of excellence. We do not assert that these are the only aspects of excellence, but we do contend that if one can attend to these five core elements consistently, one has, in earnest, begun the journey toward excellence.

Storytelling can be an entertaining and powerful way of presenting new information or reinforcing what has been learned. Therefore, we chose to personify as characters the qualities of Excellence and Average, along with their respective teams, using narrative to tell the story about the elusive yet attainable quality of excellence. We believe that this creates a unique and interesting format to best explain how to restore excellence and remove the barriers that stop us from giving and getting our best. However, this style of narration presents a challenge for the reader in differentiating the personified traits that represent Excellence from the ways in which the words are used in normal, everyday conversation. To help with this, we have capitalized the *personified* traits (Excellence, Average, etc.) and used lowercase for the normal, everyday usage of the words (excellence, average, etc.).

Too often, both at home and at work, our perception of excellence is unknowingly compromised by the insidious creep of circumstance, rationalization, and duplicity that resets the yardstick by which we measure our performance. We become inured to our circumstances and environment and fail to recognize that average has displaced excellence. *Who Kidnapped Excellence?* will cause you to look in the mirror and truthfully evaluate yourself. Once you have come face-to-face with your own reality, you can then draw from Dave's journal and the other lessons in this book to make practical changes in your life.

1

Excellence Kidnapped

*a*s Dave drove to his first delivery of the day, a sense of foreboding came over him when he saw in the distance a flashing red-and-blue glow cutting through the morning fog. When he got closer, he could see police cars sitting askew in front of Gorman-Scott Inc., their driver's-side doors still open. He got out of his delivery van and rushed toward the front doors to talk with Darnell, the corporate assistant, and see what was going on.

A policeman suddenly stepped out of the morning mist into Dave's path and said sharply, "Just a minute. Who are you, and where do you think you are going?"

"What's happened?" Dave asked, both concerned and excited. "Is everyone all right?"

"I'll ask the questions here," the policemen replied. Dave noticed another policeman putting up the yellow "Do Not Cross" crime tape so familiar from television crime shows. Eyeing Dave suspiciously, the first policeman asked again, more loudly this time, "So, who are you?"

"My name is Dave. I'm a deliveryman. I've been delivering packages here for years."

"I noticed you were limping. Is it from a recent injury?" the policeman asked.

"No!" Dave replied in surprise. "It's an old injury."

What he didn't tell the policemen was that his limp was the result of his high-tech titanium prosthetic. He had lost his right leg below the knee in a roadside bombing during his Gulf War tour. Dave didn't like to talk about his injury, and he didn't allow it to slow him down. A former marine, he had gained a reputation as an outstanding deliveryman employed by one of the world's largest package-delivery services.

Frustrated, Dave said, "Look, I have friends in there. I just want to make sure—" He was interrupted by a voice calling to them. Looking up, he saw Darnell in the front entrance, waving to him.

"Officer," she yelled, "let him in! He's OK. I'll be responsible for him."

Still looking at Dave suspiciously, the officer finally stepped aside.

As Dave and Darnell walked together toward the administrative office, he asked, "What's happened? Are you all right?"

"I'm fine," she replied. Then, glancing around as if frightened to be overheard, she whispered, "Our Excellence has been kidnapped."

"Excellence was kidnapped? What are you talking about?" Dave asked, confused.

"The ransom note was on the administrative conference room table. Found it myself this morning."

"Ransom note?" Dave was so focused on Darnell that he didn't notice a man and woman standing near the administrative office, and he walked right into them. "I am so sorry," he said.

"No problem," the man replied.

As he resumed walking with Darnell, Dave said, "They seem concerned."

Looking back, she said, "Oh, that's Jared and Jenna."

"So you were telling me about the ransom note."

"Yeah, a ransom note," she said. As they reached her desk, Darnell opened the top drawer, unfolded a piece of paper, and handed it to Dave. "I made a copy," she said. "The police have the original."

Dave took the paper and read:

Dave turned the paper over, expecting to see more, but it was blank. There was nothing else to explain what the message could mean.

Just then, a man entered the administrative office suite wearing a wrinkled, tan overcoat, looking as if he hadn't slept or shaved in days, and smelling of cigar smoke. He flashed a badge and stated curtly, "I'm Agent McNally. I need to interview Leadership."

McNally was short and stocky but exuded an authoritative, no-nonsense attitude.

"Yes, sir," Darnell replied. "Would you like to use the conference room? I'll call Leadership in right away." McNally nodded. She pointed to a door on their right and said, "This way to the conference room, sir."

He left the room, and before Darnell could follow him, Dave tapped her lightly on the shoulder.

"You mind if I sit down for a few minutes?" he asked quietly. "Leg's aching a bit," he added, rubbing his knee.

"Not at all," she replied. "Make yourself at home."

Dave sat down in the comfortable chair behind the desk in Darnell's cubicle. He slipped off his prosthesis and massaged his leg. Sighing deeply, he tried to relax his shoulders and neck. He was confused about what was happening at Gorman-Scott Inc., where he had made deliveries for years, but he felt relieved that no one he knew seemed in danger at present. As for Excellence, Dave couldn't place her and wasn't sure if he had ever met her.

After a few minutes, he heard the sounds of people entering the adjacent room and chairs being pulled out as

Leadership, Agent McNally, and Darnell took their seats around the conference table.

"McNally's the name," the agent began in a deep voice, "Agent John McNally."

As Dave heard Darnell and Leadership finish the introductions, he soon realized that he was in what could be an awkward position. He didn't want to stand up and leave, because he feared that the sound going through the open door of the conference room would interrupt the conversation that had just started. And as he sat there, he became very interested in what was being said. Part of him knew he should just risk it and get up and go, but he found himself staying in spite of his intention to leave, hoping that part of the ensuing mystery would be solved. Who was this Excellence, and why had she been kidnapped?

In the conference room, McNally asked, "How long has Excellence worked here?"

"Must be four—no five—years," Darnell answered. "I was at the first meeting Leadership had with Excellence. She came with glowing recommendations and an impressive résumé."

McNally asked, "So when did you become aware that your Excellence was missing?"

Leadership said, "We found the ransom note this morning. Hadn't realized that she was missing."

Darnell cleared her throat and said hesitantly, "I took the liberty of copying it. The officer who first arrived has the original, but here is the copy. I was careful not to leave any fingerprints or touch the original."

There was a long, pregnant pause; Dave wondered if the agent was looking at Darnell, possibly with suspicion, and he felt anxious for his friend.

Then he heard McNally slowly read the ransom note aloud: " 'We have taken your Excellence. If you ever want to see your Excellence again, open your eyes and pay the ransom.' How do you think the kidnappers got access to her? Do you know what 'open your eyes' is referring to?"

Darnell answered, "No, I don't understand it at all. I found the note around 7:30 this morning. I came into this room to make sure it was ready for an eight a.m. meeting, and it was right there on the table."

"Has anyone contacted you, giving you further information, threatening you, or asking for money to return your Excellence?" McNally inquired.

"No," Leadership and Darnell replied in unison.

"Soooo," McNally said, "can you describe this Excellence? Does she have any distinguishing characteristics? Can you give me any information that will help me to recognize her?"

Darnell and Leadership looked at each other. Darnell turned to McNally and stated, "You know, she's the best."

He stared blankly at her, and before he could put together a response, Leadership stated, "We think it would be best if we told you about her team. Excellence spends a lot of time with them."

"Team?"

"Our Excellence has a very close-knit, important team of five," Leadership replied in a tone that seemed to suggest that McNally should already have this information.

"There's Passion, Competency, Flexibility, Communication, and Ownership."

Suddenly, the conference room phone jangled loudly. Darnell jumped, and her hand flew to her mouth to stifle a scream. She pulled herself together quickly and picked up the phone. "Gorman-Scott Inc.—this is Darnell," she said. She listened quietly for a moment. Then she handed the phone to Leadership.

After listening to the caller for a few moments, Leadership stated, "Be right there," and hung up. "Something's come up," Leadership said apologetically. "Sorry, but this needs to be taken care of now. Darnell, please brief Agent McNally on Excellence's team." Looking at the agent, he said, "Anything you need, McNally, just let me know."

McNally shot Leadership a suspicious glance, wondering what could be more important than their Excellence being kidnapped. "Please don't leave the building, Leadership," he said firmly. "I may want to speak with you again."

Leadership nodded and left the room. Rushing out of the administrative office, he didn't even notice Dave sitting in Darnell's chair.

Dave glanced around. Seeing no one, he surreptitiously moved the chair closer to the door. "In for a penny, in for a pound," he said to himself.

"Well, Passion," he heard Darnell begin, "she's quite interesting."

"How so?" asked McNally.

"She is always so positive. Her main job is to inspire our employees, to make sure they know how important their jobs are and that they have a voice. Passion's role is to help our customers see that we are enthusiastic about our work, about what we produce, and that we . . . well, that we care!"

"Must be pretty energetic," McNally said.

"Oh, she is," Darnell said, nodding vigorously.

After a pause, she said, "Next is Competency, who is a key member of Excellence's team. She ensures that all of our employees are skilled in their work."

"Sounds like a full-time job," McNally offered.

"Yes, it absolutely is," Darnell agreed. "Because if our employees aren't skilled in their work, then the products and services we deliver won't meet the customers' expectations."

"Doesn't seem like rocket science," he said evenly.

Darnell stated, perhaps a bit defensively, "When most people talk about competency, they are referencing the technical skills of a particular job, but our Competency is also charged with helping our employees with the interpersonal skills so necessary to delivering great customer service."

"Got it," McNally said, writing in his notebook. "So, we have Passion and Competency. Check."

"Yes," Darnell said. "Next is Flexibility, and he is a key team member, too. Our business is constantly changing. We have new technology, new processes, new competitors, and a crazy economy. It's easy for us to become victims of our own success—to become stagnant and complacent. With so many changes, we can't get caught in the 'That's the way we've always done it' trap. We need policies, procedures, and standardization when it makes sense, but we must have Flexibility so that we are prepared to respond to unique customer situations when they occur. You see, Excellence ties all this together."

"Remind me," McNally said, "what is your position here?"

"Corporate assistant."

"You seem to know a lot about this business for a corporate assistant."

Darnell smiled and said, "I've been around a long time."

"Leadership mentioned Communication," McNally stated.

"Oh yes. She's a key member of the team. She makes sure everyone understands clearly what's expected of them, but that's not all. She has taught us a very important principle: that we must listen to everyone, especially our customers. It's amazing. We have learned that if we carefully listen to everyone—customers, employees, and others we deal with—then they can actually help us improve our business."

"They need to give you a raise," McNally stated, chuckling.

"That would be nice!" Darnell exclaimed. "I am in a position where I get to be closely involved with Leadership, management, and the line employees, so I have a unique opportunity to see things from several perspectives."

She paused to think for a moment and then continued, "Ownership—he is Excellence's other team member. He's the best! He helps us work toward a culture in which everyone takes 100 percent responsibility for their job. His role is to remind us of this. He helps us to see that sometimes we need to do things that are not necessarily in our job description but are the right course of action to take at the time. Ownership is supposed to be here, but he hasn't shown up yet."

"So, where is Excellence's team right now?" McNally asked. "Where are Passion, Competency, Flexibility, Communication, and Ownership?"

At that moment, the outer door to the conference room closed quietly. Surprised and a bit frustrated, Dave wondered if McNally had noticed that someone could be listening to the conversation. He rolled his chair closer but could hear only the low hum of voices.

He continued to sit there, lost in thought. Suddenly, he realized that his uneasiness sitting there outside the office was not just from the fear of being caught eavesdropping. This conversation about Passion, Competency, Flexibility, Communication, and Ownership had triggered something in his memory. He now knew that subconsciously he had begun questioning his own level of excellence at work and at home.

Dave was startled when the conference room door opened, and he watched Agent McNally close his notebook and walk out of the administrative suite, not even giving Dave a glance. Soon Darnell walked into the office and up to her desk.

Dave jumped up out of the chair and said with his cheeks reddening, "I'm sorry, Darnell. I probably should have left a long time ago or at least moved away from the door. I have to admit I was interested and heard everything until the door closed. It was really impressive the way you could tell him about Excellence's team and what they do here."

Darnell blushed and said reassuringly, "No worries. I know you won't talk about this to anyone else. You have been coming and going from here for a long time now. I'm sure you've probably overheard many of our secrets."

Relieved, Dave ventured, "So what happened after the door closed? Did he tell you what they are going to do to help you find Excellence?"

"I can tell you exactly what Agent McNally said." Mimicking the agent's low voice, she said, "Well, Darnell, I have been around *organizational crime* a long time, and I can tell you that you have a huge problem here. But it's not a police problem. It's a company problem and something your Leadership has to deal with."

"And?" Dave asked.

"And he left."

Incredulous, Dave said, "That's all he had to offer you?"

"That's it."

Dave shook his head and then looked at his watch. "I wish there was something I could do to help you, but I'd better get moving, too. I've got my own excellence to deliver," he said with a smile. "Hey, keep me informed, and let me know if there is any way I can help." He turned and went out the door.

As Dave drove away, he began to think deeply about the excellence, or the lack thereof, in his own life. Little did he know how this company's experience would influence his own personal journey to excellence.

Excellence's Team

Passion

Inspires everyone with energy, enthusiasm,
and caring.

Passion's job is to create that zest inside us for life that causes us to smile even when circumstances are against us, to go that extra mile, and to see our life and work as an opportunity, not something we have to get through.

Competency

Ensures everyone has all the skills needed
to do their best.

Competency is important not just in the technical aspects of our work and lives but also in our relationships with one another.

Flexibility

Helps us respond to unique situations
whenever they occur.

The only thing that remains constant is that everything changes. Flexibility understands this and helps employees to deal with and manage these changes in a practical and professional manner.

Communication

Clearly communicates roles and expectations.

Perception is everything, and perception is created by Communication. Communication respects that there is a delicate balance between listening and talking.

Ownership

Ensures everyone gives their best and takes
100 percent responsibility for their jobs.

Ownership is a personal value that promotes the knowledge that we have power and influence when we accept our responsibilities. Even in the face of constraints and barriers, we have the choice to operate using our judgment.

2

The Demand for the Return of Excellence

Leadership called an emergency meeting of Excellence's team. From their conversation as they waited for the meeting to start, it was evident that the team was in denial about Excellence's kidnapping.

"I thought I saw Excellence just last week," Competency said.

"So did I," Flexibility added without much enthusiasm.

Leadership called for silence and then addressed the team. "As much as we would like to believe that Excellence is still here with us, we obviously have a large problem.

Looking more closely at Passion, Leadership noticed that she didn't look at all like herself. Her normal vibrant color had faded—in fact, she was pale. Competency looked dazed, and Flexibility appeared stiff. Communication was silent. Ownership was missing.

After a long, awkward silence, Competency said, "I'm confused. What do they mean, 'If you ever want to see your Excellence again'? Do they expect us to pay a ransom for something we already have?"

Passion said in a voice that seemed somehow disconnected, "This is probably just a hoax. If not, let's just throw some money at the problem, and everybody will get what they want." She added, "And who would do something like this?"

Flexibility slammed his fist down on the table, causing everyone in the room to jump, and blurted out, "We will never bend to their demands!"

Communication cleared her throat and leaned forward in her chair. The team looked eagerly at her, but then she sat back, saying nothing.

"Where is Ownership?" Leadership asked irritably. Everyone just looked at one another as if searching for an answer and then shrugged their shoulders.

Just then, Ownership entered the room and quietly took his chair across from Leadership.

"Where have you been?" demanded Leadership.

"At the hospital," Ownership replied with a hint of embarrassment.

"The hospital?" Passion inquired. "What happened?"

Looking down, Ownership said in a quiet voice, "It's Performance. He has fallen again."

At this, everyone fell silent. Leadership became very still. After a few moments, he stood up and began pacing the room, finally saying, "Performance has been falling routinely for the last several months." Leadership turned to Ownership and handed a copy of the ransom note to him.

Ownership read the note and then looked up at Leadership.

Leadership asked, "So, have you seen Excellence lately?"

Ownership looked down and didn't answer.

Suddenly Leadership said loudly and emphatically, "We need to get our Excellence back! We need a plan to return her to our organization first thing in the morning. If you can't give your best, then you don't belong here. Do you understand?"

3

Average and His Team Get to Work

*a*verage was thinking about how much he was enjoying being a part of Gorman-Scott Inc., wandering the halls and hanging out in the break room. He liked it when people mistook him for Excellence. It validated his skill as a makeup artist. He was now present in every part of the company, from customer interactions to meetings, product fulfillment, and administration, and even in interpersonal matters. Average could not believe how easy it had been for him to kidnap Excellence at Gorman-Scott Inc. and replace her with himself without anyone noticing.

When Average learned of the ransom note, he called an emergency meeting with his own team in the basement of Gorman-Scott Inc. He needed his team members to continue their great work to keep Excellence from returning. Looking around the room, he had a sense of pride about the team he had assembled. He had personally trained each one of them in *his* art. He was aware that some called it an *art of deception*, but Average considered himself a legitimate makeup artist and enjoyed putting an Average face on Gorman-Scott Inc.

Sitting around the table were his protégés. Immediately to his right was N. Ept. Average was never happier than when he was in the presence of N. Ept, who was a master at convincing the higher-ups that the return on investment for training and education was not worthwhile. Average had heard N. Ept's arguments so many times that he could repeat them word for word.

"Look," N. Ept would say with conviction, "you hire smart and talented people. Just show them the ropes. Point them in a direction. Don't waste a lot of time and money on orientation and extended training programs. In a short time, you will figure out whether they get it or not. If they do, great! If not, you will replace them with someone who does."

Average was keenly aware that employees could have a good attitude and all the other elements for excellence, but if they were not competent in their work, customers would not be pleased with the total experience of doing business with the company. The opposite was also true. An employee could be great at the technical aspects of the job, but if he or she didn't have a good attitude, the customer experience could still be easily below average.

N. Flexibility was sitting stiffly next to N. Ept. Average smiled as he recalled the day that N. Flexibility swore Flexibility as his archenemy. N. Flexibility was all about following policy and procedure; he would say, "If we're not going to follow the policies and procedures, then why have them?" Average knew that on some level, paying attention to this degree of detail could actually lead to Excellence. The reality, however, was that people often perceived such approaches as sterile and robotic.

To the right of N. Flexibility was Miss Communication. Average considered Miss Communication to be the most sophisticated of his team members. She was able to use her unique skills on multiple fronts and at all levels of the organization. From an administrative perspective, she was adept at confusing messages from Leadership about the "new and improved" programs the company was rolling out. Her ability to twist Leadership's words and meanings in the minds and perceptions of the employees was uncanny. From a day-to-day frontline perspective, her real talent lay in her ability to create unbridled confusion.

Average knew that just about anyone could give good customer service, but it took an exceptional employee to create a unique and exceptional customer experience. Miss Communication fostered the confusion that prevented this. She helped the employees to see the customers as "stupid" or "manipulators" or "unreasonable," and thus the employees treated them as such. Although Average did not claim to understand how she accomplished this unique psychological feat, he knew that the usual outcome would be an average or below-average customer experience.

Next at the round table was N. Different. What Average loved about N. Different was her chameleonlike qualities.

With these, she was able to induce a myriad of responses in employees that ranged from subtle passive-aggressive behavior to downright apathy when it came to interacting with people. She preyed upon those who talked the Excellence talk but did not walk the Excellence walk. Some years ago, Average had asked N. Different why she was so successful. She did not hesitate before responding. "I am an employee advocate," she said. "I help them to understand—how should I say?—equity. Yes, I help them to understand equity. A fair day's work for a fair day's pay, eh?"

She continued, "Why should an employee go the extra mile when the company treats them like a number? I don't mean that the company treats them unfairly in the traditional sense, but rather there is a lack of respect for the employees. It may be blatant, but more often it is subtle—disguised as superficial, meaningless incentives or manipulative management double-speak that touts the benefits of a high level of commitment to the employees but, in fact, benefits only the company." N. Different smiled and said proudly, "So I teach employees to return the disrespect."

N. Different had unique capabilities when it came to provoking employees into believing that "Average is Excellence" and was a self-proclaimed nemesis of Passion. She was an enigma to Average, yet somehow her methods worked. So many times he had seen her drive passion out of employees. She was like a hyped-up drill sergeant on the first day of boot camp. Inches from the faces of a line of new employees, she would lean in and begin her rhetoric:

"Are you required to smile?" she demanded. "No, you are not!" she said emphatically, eye-to-eye with the first employee. Moving to the next employee, she demanded, "Will you make a habit of saying 'Thank you'?" Without pause, she declared, "You will not make a habit of saying 'Thank you,' especially to the customer. You are providing them with your time, your energy, your expertise! They should be thanking you!" Moving up close to the next employee, N. Different said in a hushed but authoritative voice, "Will you ever, under any circumstance, apologize?"

This time she did not answer her own question. Finally, the employee realized that he was expected to answer and blurted out, "No, sir. I mean, ma'am."

"I can't hear you!" N. Different yelled.

"No, sir! I mean, ma'am!" the employee yelled back.

Then, pacing up and down the line, N. Different gave the speech that Average had heard so many times in so many companies. "People, especially customers, are a necessary evil. You must deal with them, but they are not your bosses and they are not your mothers. You will provide your company's service or product, but you are not obligated to be a cheerleader while you do it. You will ignore any hint of desire to go above and beyond the call of duty." She paused and then yelled, "Do I make myself clear?"

The line of employees yelled back in unison, "Yes, sir! I mean, ma'am!"

Average thought how ironic it was that N. Different could generate so much passion about not being nice to everyone, especially the customer.

The final member of Average's team, Poser, was sitting in the corner of the room instead of at the table. He was leaning back in his chair and staring at the ceiling while nursing a toothpick. Average noted that today Poser wore his flashy cowboy boots and cowboy hat, meaning that he was in a mood mainly made up of bravado. At other times, Poser wore his camouflage outfit, which signified a more subdued mood. When he was feeling wicked, Poser would put on a ventriloquist outfit of a tuxedo and bowtie, which meant that the employees were mere puppets or dummies who had their strings pulled by management. These were but three of the many characters he used to get employees to challenge his enemy, Ownership, and avoid taking responsibility. Companies might get off to a good start with initiatives that could lead to Excellence, but they needed Ownership to sustain it. Average knew that was Poser's sweet spot.

Average cleared his throat to get his team's attention. All went quiet, and Average said seriously, "We have a leak somewhere."

"A leak?" N. Different asked.

Average passed copies of the ransom note around the table. He said, nodding at Miss Communication, "Thanks to Miss Communication, this came to my attention a short time ago."

The team was dumbstruck. Each member was thinking the same thought: "Our team has always been so loyal to Average. How could any one of us betray him?" However, none of them spoke it aloud.

Average filled the void for them. "Look, I do not believe that any of you would have knowingly tipped off the organization about Excellence's kidnapping." There was a unanimous sigh of relief. "The fact of the matter is, however, Gorman-Scott Inc. is now aware of it," he said.

"What are we going to do?" N. Ept inquired.

Surprising everyone, Average stood, slammed his fists on the table, and yelled, "I'll tell you what we're going to do. You're all going to do your jobs! That's what we are going to do!" He began slowly walking around the table. Finally he said, "What is it that we do?"

Miss Communication started to speak but stopped when Average raised his hand. He continued, "What we do is lull organizations into complacency, and that, my friends, leads to the holy grail of average: bad customer experiences and falling performance.

"What we do," Average said with added emphasis, "is get companies to unknowingly lower their standards. Then they start to believe that I, Average, am, in fact, Excellence! In short, we deceive organizations."

Still standing, he leaned forward, placed his hands flat on the table, and said in a taunting voice, "So my question to you is this: Are you capable of producing? This is where the rubber meets the road. Each one of you has a specific job to do. Can I count on you to continue to get the job done here at Gorman-Scott Inc.?"

Together the team yelled, "Yes, you can!"

"Then let's get down to business," Average said with pride. He unveiled a whiteboard with the names of both

Excellence's team members and his own written on it, and they began to decide what they were going to do next.

EXCELLENCE'S TEAM VERSUS AVERAGE'S TEAM

Excellence	Average
Passion	N. Different
Competency	N. Ept
Flexibility	N. Flexibility
Communication	Miss Communication
Ownership	Poser

Average's Team

N. Different

Continues to deflate Passion.

N. Different's job is to destroy the zest for life inside of us. N. Different is willing to trade outcomes brought about by hard work for the path of least resistance.

N. Ept

Helps dumb down Competency.

N. Ept promotes the status quo in technical and interpersonal skills.

Miss Communication

Is always obfuscating Communication.

Miss Communication is a master of the mixed messages that promote confusion.

N. Flexibility

Constantly stiffens Flexibility.

N. Flexibility chooses policy and procedure over adaptability and common sense.

Poser

Disguises himself as Ownership

Poser simply wants to deceive and impress. Poser wants you to believe that he works harder, brings more value, and has more influence than others in the company.

4
Below Average

a twelve-by-twelve-inch sliding metal panel was situated at eye level in the only door of the small, poorly lit basement room where Excellence had been held in captivity for several months. Sitting quietly, she calmly turned toward the door as the panel began to slide open. Excellence stood up. As usual, she was taken aback by the face staring at her from the other side of the opening. There was an uncanny resemblance between Excellence and this figure. Over time, however, Excellence had begun to recognize that what had at first appeared to be subtle differences had become glaring differences. Unfortunately, she was sure that others might not be able to easily tell the difference between the two of them.

With a wry smile, the figure said, "Good morning, Excellence."

"Good morning, Average," Excellence replied in a pleasant tone that belied her situation.

Over the past months, Excellence had learned much about Average's history from these visits. In an earlier life, Average had been a makeup artist. He began his career behind the scenes of a theater company, and over the years, he became an expert in his field. He had, in fact, become obsessed with Excellence in his art, but with economic changes in the industry, he found himself a victim of downsizing and was replaced by less experienced artists. Outraged, he changed his name to Average and committed the rest of his life to keeping Excellence out of any company he could.

"Gorman-Scott Inc. has become comfortable with me," Average said slyly to Excellence, who maintained her calm demeanor and did not respond. "You've been my captive here for some time now, and they didn't even know you were gone until they received a ransom note for your return. They've been accepting me for you, and I plan to keep it that way. And my team and I will do everything in our power to make sure that I, Average, am firmly entrenched at this organization."

"They will figure it out," Excellence replied in a matter-of-fact tone.

"Will they now?" Average retorted. "Well, let me tell you what I think. I've been doing this a long time, and I have experience with thousands of companies. Here's how it works. At some point in the company's life cycle, Leadership gets focused on you, Excellence, and adopts a silly mantra, such as 'Excellence in All We Do.' A lot of excitement is generated. They have meetings, campaigns, posters, surveys, and contests. The list goes on and on. They assemble a team to support Excellence like they did at Gorman-Scott Inc. But eventually reality sets in." Average straightened his collar with pride and said, "That's when my team shows up. We help the company to understand its place in the world; it is just good enough at what it does to get by. Its customers should be grateful that the products and services are available to them."

"So, you lie to them," Excellence stated, never changing her expression.

"Oh, no, no, no!" Average exclaimed. "Such an exaggerated overstatement. 'Average' does not imply that the customer does not have a place in the process, but we help give the companies—how shall I say it?—ah, perspective. Yes, that's it. We help give them perspective."

"And that perspective is?"

"Employees work hard enough as it is. They have enough to do without spending so much time and energy on you—Excellence. Customers have no understanding of all the hard work happening behind the scenes to deliver a great product or service. The employees become happy with me. And before you know it," Average continued proudly, "I, Average, have replaced you, Excellence."

"You can put lipstick on a pig," Excellence said, smiling, "but it is still a pig."

Average sighed heavily and stroked his chin. He said, "Look, Excellence. You and I are not all that different. I think that we could be friends. It is not that I—"

"We are nothing alike," Excellence interrupted.

Average was intrigued. He sensed that Excellence was angry, yet she never lost her smile, nor did her tone show any evidence of anger.

"We are nothing alike," Excellence said again. "Our standards are different, and our perspectives on what a company should be and do are not even close. You see the employee as a pawn in a business chess game, a pawn that can be moved around and perhaps even sacrificed to meet the needs of the leaders. You see employees as people to be manipulated, as individuals who don't care about one other and have no desire to strive to be their best. And you see a customer as someone to be taken advantage of. I, on the other hand, believe that employees want to be their best, to be more like me, Excellence. Also, I see the customer as the reason we are in business and the focus of all we do, not only as some unfortunately necessary part. And the measure of how well we are meeting everyone's wants, needs, and desires is the deciding factor in whether Gorman-Scott Inc. is creating great customer experiences." Excellence paused and then said, "Friends, you say. What a joke. We will never be friends! Have you ever heard author Jim Collins's phrase, 'Good is the enemy of great'?"

Before Average could reply, Excellence stated emphatically, *"Average is the enemy of being your best."*

"Have it your way," Average sneered. "But let me leave you with this thought. You've been locked away in this basement for months in this basement under the very company where you once thrived. Has anyone sent out a rescue team? No! And while you waste away down here,

my team and I are walking the floors over your head."
Average burst out laughing and said, "You think you're so
high and mighty, but I am actually above you. So, in reality, Excellence is below Average. Get it? Below Average!"

Excellence turned her back on Average, as the familiar metallic sound of the panel closing told her the conversation was over—for now. Excellence smiled, and the
smile slowly widened because she knew that Average had
not taken time to understand who she really was and that
he was operating under false assumptions.

"He defines me as being above the fiftieth percentile,"
Excellence said to herself. "That's his first mistake. I am
not defined by a comparison with my colleagues, peers,
or friends. I am defined by a comparison of my current
status with my potential, my best! Do I have standards
and expectations related to my employment? Yes, I do!
Do I have roles and responsibilities to fulfill in my family
life? Certainly! But those are the minimum requirements
to keep my job and my relationships. My best—now, that
comes from inside and is not always measurable in others'
eyes. But I know when I've given it, and I know when I
have given just enough to stay under the radar.

"Average's second mistake is underestimating my ability to bounce back. Everyone has a bad day at work or
at home now and again. I am no exception, but I don't
let those days define me. My Passion, Competency,
Flexibility, Communication, and Ownership are . . . well,
they are mine. These are who make up my team. They
define me. Their qualities are inside me, and to use them
positively is my choice day by day, minute by minute."

Excellence was keenly aware of the cunning of Average. Average knew that all five of Excellence's team members had to operate at optimal levels for Excellence to be released, and like a predator hunting a pack, Average had to keep at least one or two members down to stay alive and make sure that Excellence was subdued.

Average's words came back to Excellence: "You've been my captive here for some time now, and they didn't even know you were gone until they received a ransom note for your return." This was Average's third mistake: not recognizing the significance that someone had noticed—and not knowing that collective, organizational excellence happens one person at a time, and that the realization of the absence of Excellence is the first step of recovery.

She knew that her team had been made aware of her absence and that they would do everything they could to get her back. She also had a good idea of who had sent the ransom note.

5

Passion Meets
N. Different

L eadership's team met for hours to develop a plan to get Excellence back. The conversations were direct and stressful, but still a definitive plan had not materialized. Passion left the meeting feeling listless. She went to her office and closed the door. Pulling out her compact mirror, she looked closely at herself. "I'm so pale," she thought. "What's happened to me? I used to be so full of feeling, warmth, and zeal." Then her phone rang, and Passion answered it. "Yes," she said, and even to her own ears, her voice sounded empty of life.

It was Darnell. "You have a visitor here to see you," she said.

Passion had very few visitors. "Who is it?" she asked with interest.

"She says she is a family member," Darnell replied.

Passion racked her brain but could not think of what family member might be visiting her at work. "Send her to my office, please," Passion finally said.

Moments later a woman entered and hugged Passion halfheartedly. Before her, Passion saw a woman who seemed to have some of the family characteristics, but she could not place her. The visitor seemed to read her mind.

"We've actually never met face-to-face," the woman said. "My name is N. Different. Perhaps your parents told you about me?" she added, sitting down. "Third cousin once removed."

Passion sat down across from her. Her parents had certainly told her about this woman. Actually, her parents had warned her about N. Different.

Again, N. Different seemed to read her thoughts. She said, smiling, "Look, none of those childhood stories are true. I've heard them all, too. 'Watch out for N. Different. She's no good. She'll suck the life out of you. She'll leave you cold, empty, and wasted.'" Suddenly, N. Different laughed in a way that was almost maniacal.

"What are you doing here? What do you want?" Passion asked skeptically.

"I am here to help you," N. Different responded, and Passion noticed that she was no longer smiling. "You don't seem to be at your best right now."

"Help with . . . ?" inquired Passion.

"Don't play coy with me," N. Different stated. "You know your Excellence is missing. Your leader has put the responsibility on you to get her back, and you are sitting here wondering what went wrong, what you could have done differently, and what you are going to do now."

"But how could you—"

"I make it my business to know," N. Different shot back. "And do you want to know what I have learned?" Not allowing Passion to answer, she continued, "I've learned that you have taken this onto your own shoulders. I've learned that you feel personally responsible for Excellence's kidnapping."

Her eyes welling with tears, Passion replied, "It's true. I don't know what happened, but I seem to have lost my spirit." Sniffling, she added, "And if I had been doing my job correctly, Excellence would still be here."

N. Different handed Passion a handkerchief and said, "There, there, dear. Tell me the whole story."

Wiping her tears away, Passion blurted out, "I'm Passion! I give enthusiasm to our employees. You see," she continued, gaining some composure, "there is more to Excellence than just the technical skills of the job. Some of our employees don't understand this truth at first. Our customers are certainly interested in getting a great product, but they also want to know that our employees care." She paused for a moment and then said, "It's how we treat and help each other; the way we look one another in the eye; the acknowledgment that we are listening to our customers' wants, needs, and concerns. It's the smile on our face and the inflection in our voice. It's helping the employees understand the need to see each customer interaction with fresh eyes.

"Do you understand," Passion said, leaning forward in her chair, "how easy it is to slip into a mundane perspective when it comes to our jobs and our customers? What I try to teach is empathy. If we are empathetic with one another, then we can be that way with our customers, and we are more likely to understand their perspective. You know the old adage about treating others the way you want to be treated? There's a lot of truth to that." She took a deep breath. With tears again running down her pale face, she said, "I create the environment for Excellence to thrive. I'm the one who carries the torch for Excellence, and I let that torch go out."

N. Different got up from her chair and walked to the window. She stared out for a long time before she turned, looked directly at Passion, and said, as if talking to a child, "You do your job well enough. You explain your importance at each new-employee orientation. You make it clear that you, Passion, are an essential function of their jobs." She stated matter-of-factly, "You're done—nothing more you can do. You can't babysit these people. You do your best, and either they get it or they don't."

"But—" Passion began.

"No buts!" N. Different declared. "And don't forget," she said conspiratorially, "you have plenty of other team members who need to do their jobs. There's Competency, Flexibility, Communication, and Ownership. If they would do their jobs right, maybe yours wouldn't be so hard."

Passion heard what N. Different was saying, but still she wasn't convinced. Walking toward the door, N. Different said, "I have to go for now. Wouldn't your life be easier if you didn't care so much? Why waste your time? Do you think anyone else really cares? Think about what I've said. And," she added, "if you ever need me, just close your eyes and relax. I'll be there."

This time it was Passion's turn to stare out the window. She had a lot to think about.

Special Delivery: PASSION

Passion is what turns life into an adventure.
—Ed Jent

When Dave left Gorman-Scott Inc., he noticed that the parking lot had fewer cars than usual at that time of day. He had worked for Delivery LLC for almost ten years, and Gorman-Scott Inc. had been on his route for the last four. Somehow, the kidnapping of Excellence was not as big of a surprise to him as he thought it should be. Musing on this, he recalled that the number of packages he delivered there had been decreasing over the last year, and, as today, there were fewer and fewer cars in the parking lot, which meant fewer customers. The building's grounds had appeared increasingly unkempt. Now that he thought more deeply about it, he realized that Gorman-Scott Inc.'s entire character had changed. Not a dramatic, earth-moving change, but a subtle and ill-defined change that was nevertheless present and palpable.

Dave's thoughts turned to his own company and then to himself. His company had Passion. He had seen a lot of her at first, and he remembered how, after he had become acquainted with her, she began to approach every day, every situation, and every customer with enthusiasm and fresh eyes. He remembered the story that Passion had told to the group during orientation about her dog.

"I want you all to adopt the Dooley philosophy," she said, smiling.

THE DOOLEY PHILOSOPHY
One should live one's life seeing every opportunity as new and exciting

Passion went on to explain that her dog's name was Dooley, and Dooley went out the same door several times a day to do his business and explore the backyard. "And if you could read Dooley's body language," she said, "and the way his eyes widen and his body trembles with antici-pation, it's like the first time he's ever been out that door each and every time, and he can't wait to get out there and explore."

Passion's story struck a chord with Dave and became part of his mental and emotional toolbox, the one he tried to pull from as he dealt with life's daily challenges and set-backs. On the days when he dealt with pain or struggled to do his daily tasks with his prosthesis in place, his world would feel dark and his mind would retreat back to the day he lost his lower leg. The Dooley philosophy was one of the concepts that helped him emerge from the gloom to brightness and hope. But, Dave realized, it had been a long while since he had thought about this particular way of viewing the world.

Additionally, Dave's job had become too comfortably routine. He knew his customers, and they knew him. But as he thought about his customer interactions, he realized that their conversations had eroded into banalities: How are the kids? How's the wife? The job? These pleasantries were all well and good, but suddenly Dave realized that somewhere along the way he had stopped paying attention—that is, he had stopped really listening. He wasn't seeing his customers with *fresh* eyes, and he was operating on automatic. He had abandoned the Dooley philosophy. He was not giving or getting his best.

And then Dave experienced the real epiphany. It came so hard and fast that he had to slow his breathing. The same thoughts he was having about his job—the routine, the ordinary, the feigned pleasantries, the not seeing with fresh eyes—these same things were true of his marriage.

Over the last few years, he and Mary had drifted apart. It wasn't something they really talked about. Correct that—it wasn't something *he* talked about. She had tried to discuss it with him many times, but each time, either he was able to redirect the conversation or the discussion ended in anger and silence. He still loved Mary. Trying to recall their passion, he came to realize that somewhere along the way, she had quit trying so hard and their marriage was now more of an arrangement bound by financial circumstances, a shared history, and love for the children they had together. But where was the passion now?

6

Competency
Meets N. Ept

*a*fter the Leadership team meeting, Competency went to the ladies' room to splash her face with cool water and attempt to relieve her stress. "What have I been doing?" she thought. "Have I in some way contributed to this situation? My job is to ensure that our employees are at their best in their technical work and in how they interact with customers. We have a decent orientation program, and I connect every new employee with a mentor. The budget has been tightening over the past few years, and it seems as if I am the first one they come to for cost reductions. Have I compromised for the sake of Excellence? Maybe I have not paid enough attention to Excellence in our training initiatives. Perhaps I have failed to set up the correct expectations concerning how we deal with customers and with each other."

Looking into the mirror and drying her face, she said aloud, "But Excellence's kidnapping is not my fault."

"That's right," the reflection in the mirror calmly said, "It's not your fault."

Startled, Competency wiped her eyes again and peered more closely into the mirror. What she saw staring back was a likeness of herself. However, the image was distorted. Attributing the occurrence to the fact that she was feeling stressed and upset, she tapped lightly on the mirror and smiled.

The image did not smile back.

"You're not hallucinating," N. Ept said, again startling Competency.

"Who are you?" Competency demanded.

"My name is N. Ept. But that's not important," she said coolly. "What's important is that your last statement was correct. It's not your fault."

"But—" began Competency.

"Now, now," interrupted N. Ept. "You do not give yourself enough credit." She knew she had Competency's attention and offered empathetically, "You can only do so much."

"I do work hard," Competency asserted.

"Certainly you work hard," N. Ept agreed. "But you can't control everything. You have boundaries established by the higher-ups, do you not?" Competency nodded in agreement, and N. Ept continued, "You barely have the resources to get the employees to know the technical aspects of their jobs. And shouldn't employees understand how to create great customer experiences? I mean, it's not that hard."

"But our Excellence is missing in every aspect of our business, and it shows most clearly in customer service," Competency said with concern.

N. Ept smiled. "She's not missing. They're trying to distract you from your real job. Just go back and do what you do every day. You don't deserve this stress. You're doing the best you can under the circumstances."

Competency ran the water in the sink and splashed her face again. When she looked up at the mirror, all she saw was her own reflection.

Special Delivery: COMPETENCY

Avoid competency traps. Do not stay only where you are good at things. Go out and be challenged. —Andrew Creighton

The next day, Dave practiced his renewed Dooley philosophy. He was at Anderson Inc., his next-to-last stop of the day, and Mrs. Gonzalez was signing for their packages. "How are the children?" Dave asked cheerfully. "You have two, correct? Forgive me, but their names escape me."

"Juan and Christina. They are doing OK," Mrs. Gonzalez said, not meeting Dave's eyes. It seemed to him that she was holding something back.

In the past, he would have said something nice, thanked her, and left. Instead, he said tentatively, "You seem down."

Mrs. Gonzalez reached for a tissue from her desk and wiped away a tear. Finally, she said, "I admit, I'm struggling right now. I've been the administrative assistant here for almost a year, and . . . and my annual evaluation is next week, and I don't think it's going to go well."

Dave was acutely aware of time. One of the core competencies of his job was getting packages to customers on schedule. He had only one more delivery today. Quickly he glanced at the clock on the wall and was relieved to find that he had a few minutes to talk with Mrs. Gonzalez and still get the last package delivered on time.

"I don't get along so well with two of the senior management people," she admitted, her cheeks turning red.

As he and Mrs. Gonzalez spoke together, Dave quickly realized that she had two areas where she could improve. One was the technical aspect: what she was to do, how to do it, and when to do it. The other concerned her interpersonal relationships with the many people she interacted with. He did not feel qualified to give her advice regarding the technical aspects of her job except for encouraging her to find the right resources, training, guidance, and support systems to improve, but he did have advice about her relationships. "Who do you consider to be your customers?" he asked her cheerfully.

The question obviously took her by surprise. "Customers?" she repeated.

"Yeah. Who do you consider *your* customers?"

Mrs. Gonzalez thought for a moment. Finally, she said, "Well, the people who buy our products and services. They are our customers."

"But that wasn't my question," Dave said lightly. "My question was, who are your customers?"

Before she could answer, he said, "Let me tell you a story that my boss told me many years ago. What he learned from the situation he told about had a strong effect on him, and it has certainly influenced me."

Mrs. Gonzalez smiled and said, "Please, anything you can do to help will be appreciated."

"Some years ago," Dave began, "my boss was working on his graduate degree in management. He was working full time and going to school at night. One evening the professor told the class that he was going to show them how Japanese management philosophies define the word *customer*."

Mrs. Gonzalez, clearly intrigued, said, "And?"

"The professor simply said that they see the customer as the next person in the process," he continued.

"'The next person in the process?" Mrs. Gonzalez repeated, looking puzzled.

"Yeah, and the professor went on to tell the students that their assignment was to go back to where they worked and identify a process that was not working well. And instead of viewing the next person in the process that was not working as a problem or a barrier, the students were instructed to view this person as a customer and to ask the person in that context to help them improve the outcome of the process."

"Very interesting," Mrs. Gonzalez said.

"Wait until you hear this!" Dave said. "My boss knew exactly what he was going to do. And remember, this was a long time ago—long before there was e-mail. He was in middle management then, and he had nine departments that reported to him. The major form of written communication at the time was the memo."

Mrs. Gonzalez laughed. "Hey, that wasn't all that long ago."

"My boss said his issue was that he would dictate his memos, and there was an administrative assistant, Claudia, who transcribed them. He said he had never gotten a correctly transcribed memo back the first time."

"Really, never?" Mrs. Gonzalez said with disbelief.

"Yes. And so he sat down with Claudia, stated the problem, and informed her that he was now seeing her as his customer. He then asked her if she would, as his customer, help him solve this problem."

"I am impressed. How did she respond?"

"Now we come to the pinnacle of the story," Dave said excitedly. "Claudia looked him straight in the eye and stated emphatically that he mumbled, which made it difficult for her to understand him."

"You are kidding me," Mrs. Gonzalez said.

"No, I am not kidding," Dave responded. "But that's not the entire story. You see, my boss worked in the chemical industry back then, and his undergraduate degree was in chemistry. Claudia went on to tell my boss that she did not have a chemistry degree like he did, so when he dictated a complex chemical name, couldn't he just spell it out for her?"

"She didn't."

"She did," Dave replied. "And do you know what happened?"

"What?"

"The error rate went down to almost zero, starting that day," Dave said proudly, as if it had been his accomplishment.

"That's amazing," Mrs. Gonzalez said.

"So," Dave offered, "too often, we confine our definition of the customer to the one who is buying the product or service. We need to broaden it to this:

The customer is the next person in the process.

He continued, "Then our perspective of customer-service excellence would be enhanced. So, when I asked you who your customers were, I was wondering whether you were considering those two senior management people to be your customers."

"I've never thought about it like that," she said.

"I can't help you with the technical aspects of your job," Dave said, "but this is a way of thinking that may help you. If you can develop a way of seeing 'the next person in the process' as your customer, then you can give them your best. When you approach them from that perspective, communication begins to flow. I encourage you to sit down with the two senior management people you mentioned, tell them that you view them as your customers, and invite them to tell you what you can do to better serve them."

"Wow!" Mrs. Gonzalez stated, wide-eyed. "I'll do it!"

Shaking her hand, Dave said, "I need to go. Let me know how it goes."

"I will," Mrs. Gonzalez said, smiling, "And thank you, Dave. Thank you for taking the time to help me."

As he was driving to his last drop of the day, Dave looked in the rearview mirror and thought, "I'd better start practicing what I am preaching. It's easy to tell someone else to view and treat others from a customer perspective. Mary's the most important next person in the process in my life, but I have failed to treat her as such."

He glanced again in the rearview mirror and said out loud, "I hope she can forgive me. I can only hope she will. I can't lose her. I will ask for her forgiveness tonight." And, he thought, "I will commit to giving her my best in the future."

7

Flexibility Meets
N. Flexibility

flexibility was doing some reflecting of his own but in a much different manner. As he sat on the floor of his office in the lotus position, Flexibility sank deep into a transcendental meditative state. He believed he had reached the level of enlightenment. His mind was clear, and his thoughts flowed as if he were conversing with himself. "Flexibility, you must go back to the basics to get Excellence back. You have done a fairly good job of defining our employees' roles and responsibilities in their work, and creating policies and procedures about how to operate our business, but you have failed to create an infrastructure or, perhaps better said, a platform where employees can use their own judgment and common sense in situations that do not fit the mold.

"What if the solution to your issues and problems might be found in listening to the people involved in the process rather than trying to solve it with a policy? What if you were always to provide the relevant people the opportunity to be involved in solving the problem? What if you created a culture that encouraged your employees to know and understand your policies but gave them the freedom to bend the policies in unique situations? You could teach them to adhere to the core principles of a great customer experience even if it departed somewhat from your normal policies. Certainly, you must create some boundaries, but you have some smart and talented people here. You ought to show a little respect and give them a little credit and latitude.

"What if you were always to provide the relevant people the opportunity to be involved in solving the problem?"

"Careful now. You're going to strain something there," a voice said from seemingly far away. Flexibility opened his eyes and was startled to see a man standing over him with the most ramrod-straight posture he had ever seen.

Flexibility took a deep breath and looked up at the man from his lotus position. "Can I help you?" he asked politely but somewhat guardedly.

"Seems to me that you may be about to stretch beyond your capabilities," the man said dispassionately.

Unfurling from his position, Flexibility replied, "I'm not sure what you are talking about. I am very limber." He hesitated and then said, "Who are you, anyway?"

"Oh, I didn't mean you personally," N. Flexibility said. "I was referring to your employees and you asking them to use their own judgment and common sense. Even you know that's a bit of a stretch," he said, smiling now. "And it's a fairly major risk, if you want my opinion."

Getting up, Flexibility began, "How did you—"

N. Flexibility interrupted with a wave of his hand, "It doesn't matter how I know what you were thinking. I'm just here to help, to prevent you from making a major error in judgment."

N. Flexibility's demeanor was so matter-of-fact and his posture was so upright that Flexibility forgot about caring who he was. He inquired, "Major error in judgment?"

"I understand you received a ransom note for your Excellence."

"Yes," Flexibility replied.

"Well, I can understand how you might take that personally," N. Flexibility said. "The biggest mistake you can make right now," he asserted with authority, "is to overreact. If you start allowing your employees to 'do their own thing,' even if you think you put in appropriate boundaries, well . . . " He laughed sarcastically.

"But—" Flexibility began.

"Use your common sense!" N. Flexibility declared. "You have good policies and procedures. Follow them. You are not responsible for the kidnapping of Excellence."

"We cannot ignore that Performance has fallen here!" Flexibility said.

"I'm not asking you to," N. Flexibility replied. "But I think you owe it to yourself to look for the reason for Performance's fall. Let me tell what you're going to find," he said. "You're going to find issues related to the economy. You're going to find flaws with suppliers who are adding to your costs. You're going to find increased regulatory changes adding undue pressure to your operations. You need to operate in the real world," he said emphatically. "These are cold, hard issues affecting your Performance. You are too soft! If you give your employees enough rope, they are not going to find Excellence and lasso her in. What they are going to do is hang themselves, and the company too."

Flexibility was getting angry. He closed his eyes and counted to ten, a technique he had learned to control his anger. When he opened them, he was alone. "Could he be correct?" thought Flexibility. "I mean, the economy, our suppliers, the regulatory changes, they really are outside of my control." Flexibility quickly realized that Leadership would not accept this type of rationalization. He closed his eyes again. "I must look inside for the solution," he said softly. "I will not make excuses. I will be part of the solution."

Special Delivery: FLEXIBILITY

*I'm looking for a few good men with an
infinite capacity for not knowing what cannot
be done. —Henry Ford*

After Dave resolved to restore his relationship with his wife, his thoughts transitioned to a deep sense of pride because he had been able to help Mrs. Gonzalez. He hoped she would follow through with the plan to talk to her superiors. When he neared his last drop of the day, Dave noticed that he had a text message. It was his supervisor asking him to come in at six the next morning, much earlier than usual. After reading it, he felt a hot flush of anger, but it passed quickly. He remembered that flexibility was an important aspect of excellence. His supervisor rarely asked him to go above and beyond the call of duty, and when he did ask, Dave tried hard to respond positively. "Glad to," he replied to the message.

In an instant he received a text back from his supervisor. It read, "U R the Best!"

"The best?" Dave mused. "I'm not so sure about that." His mind drifted back to the idea of Flexibility. He mused, "It's a lot easier to be flexible at work than in my personal life." He was thinking of his family's recent vacation to Disney World, a trip almost ruined because of his inflexibility. He had planned out everything perfectly, but he hadn't expected three days of rain. The whole time they were stuck indoors, Mary kept saying, "Look, we can't control the weather. Let's just play it by ear and go with the flow."

But Dave was used to things being on schedule. His job required it, and the need for control had drifted into his personal life. During the rainy days of the trip, the tension had become so great that Mary sent Katherine and Jonathan to the hotel's indoor pool so that she could talk with Dave.

She said to him, "Dave, if you don't learn to roll with the punches, you're going to have high blood pressure."

"But I—"

Mary held up her hand, stopping him. "Not only are you going to damage your health," she said, "but also you're setting a bad example for the kids."

Dave softened at this and said, "I'm sorry." Then he began to really listen.

"I love your sense of organization," she said, patting him on the back. "It is a wonderful trait, and in many ways it keeps us on track. But you are going to have to loosen up when things do not go according to plan, when circumstances are outside your control."

"I know," Dave replied.

"It's not a sign of weakness," Mary offered. "In fact, to understand that you are not in control of everything and to be able to adapt to barriers and disappointments is actually a sign of strength."

"I never thought of it like that," he replied. Taking his wife by the hand, he said, smiling, "I'm going to do better with this, but I need your help."

"You got it!" she replied eagerly. "We'll need a code word or a phrase. If I sense that you are becoming inflexible on something important and feel you should pull back and reevaluate, I will say, 'Why don't you take time out to stretch a bit. I think that will make you feel better.' How does that sound?"

"Too complicated," Dave replied, smiling. "Just give me that look you give me sometimes and say, 'Stretch, Dave.' I'll get it."

"That sounds good," she said, as she kissed him on the cheek.

"What do you say we get our bathing suits on and join the kids?" Dave suggested. "The Magic Kingdom can wait another day or two for us!"

It now struck Dave that that week had ultimately been a good one in regard to his marriage. "Where did things go wrong?" he thought. "What was different about that week compared with the others, when I felt so disconnected from Mary?" Holding back tears, he said out loud, "I have to figure out how to get back to that connection."

8

Communication Meets Miss Communication

Communication had hardly said a word at the meeting with Leadership. Now, in her own office, she put on noise-reducing headphones and looked out the window, in which she could see her faint reflection. No music played. She just needed silence, silence to think.

"What has happened to my concentration?" she wondered. "I used to be much better at it. I could listen intently. I listened with my brain, my eyes, and my ears. I picked up on body language. I maintained eye contact, and I was able to truly understand what everyone was saying. And I was articulate when it was time for me to speak. I made my message personal. I made sure that everyone heard a message that was clear and easily understood. And no one ever walked away without understanding what the next steps would be. I could focus back then."

As she sat at her desk surrounded by silence, Communication became sleepy. Closing her eyes, she thought, "This is what I passed on to the employees—this ability to listen earnestly and speak with clarity. This is what helped bring Excellence to our company."

"Maybe. Maybe not," a soft voice whispered. At first, Communication thought she must be dreaming, so she was not startled, but then the voice said much more loudly, "You can talk yourself into just about anything if you want to believe it badly enough."

Communication opened her eyes to see a woman sitting just inches away from her. Although she was now alarmed, she could not help but notice how much the woman looked like her. The person looked like a younger and smaller version of herself.

"Who are you?" she demanded.

Smiling, the woman replied, "Name's Miss Communication. Pleasure to meet you. My friends just call me Missy. Please, you must call me Missy," she said pleasantly.

"Well, Missy," Communication said, trying to sound authoritative, "now that I know your name, what do you want? Why did you sneak up on me?"

"A bit paranoid, are we?" Missy intoned softly. "Nobody's sneaking up on you. You had your eyes closed."

"What did you mean when you said, 'Maybe. Maybe not. You can talk yourself into just about anything if you want to believe it badly enough'?"

"I was just answering you. Self-deception is a strong anesthetic," Missy said nonchalantly.

"Answering me?"

Missy chuckled. "I suppose you were talking in your sleep," she replied. "Anyway, the state that you seek does not exist."

"State? What state?" Communication asked with interest.

"The state of clarity," Missy replied earnestly. "Doesn't exist."

"Of course it exists," Communication scoffed. "I've been there many times."

Missy laughed sarcastically and said, "The only state you have been in is a state of denial."

Communication was taken aback that someone this young could be so brazen. "Now see here!" she said.

"Easy now," Missy crooned. "I'm not trying to get you angry, but I do want to make sure that I have your attention." After Communication settled back to listen, Missy continued, "I'm just here to tell you that you are putting way too much energy into this Excellence."

"Meaning?" Communication asked.

"Meaning that the messaging that results in excellence ought to come naturally—you know, spontaneously. You concern yourself with eye contact, body language, filters, biases, and ambiguity." Missy paused and then exclaimed, "Rubbish! It's all rubbish!"

"It's not!" Communication said defensively.

"I tell you it is rubbish!" Missy asserted. "What people really want is authenticity. They don't want to be around someone who is overly concerned with their body language or their eye contact. When you are constantly trying to find the exact right word for every moment, you come across as being phony. And when you come across as phony," Missy added, "you block your meaningless little quest for clarity right out of the gate."

As much as she did not like Missy, Communication could not dispute that authenticity was what most people wanted. However, she said, "You talk as if the ability to be authentic and the basic concepts of discourse are mutually exclusive or, even better said, diametrically opposed."

"Would you listen to yourself?" Missy interrupted. "You are making another point for me," she said, smiling.

"Point?" Communication inquired.

"Yes, a major point!" Mimicking Communication, she said, "'You talk as if the ability to be authentic and the basic concepts of discourse are mutually exclusive or, even better said, diametrically opposed.' Come on. Who talks like that? Save that rhetoric for the academic journals."

Communication was silent.

"Nobody talks like that," Missy continued. "Maybe more important, nobody listens to people talking like that." She suddenly seemed to check herself, and she took a different tack. "Look, the frontline people don't really care about all the rationalizations going into decisions and changes. They don't care about the business case and all this management stuff about listening to them and getting their buy-in. It's just rubbish."

Communication stared silently at Missy.

"Quit bugging them with all the details of the strategic plan, mission, vision, and values of the company," she said. "They don't care! That is management's job. The frontliners just need to know what they have to know, so that they can do their jobs and go home. Do you understand?"

Communication did not respond. It was growing dark, and she could now only see her own fading reflection in the window. She was alone. She took off her headphones. Had she been dreaming, or had she just had a conversation with Miss Communication? She shook her head back and forth quickly as if to shake the cobwebs from her brain. It didn't help; she was still unclear about what had just happened. But what was clear to her, however, was that the organization could not afford confusion. She must get Excellence back. "I am going to give it my best!" she exclaimed so loudly that she surprised herself.

Special Delivery: COMMUNICATION

*The single biggest problem with
communication is the illusion that it has
taken place. —George Bernard Shaw*

As Dave arrived at his last client's office, his mind drifted to the idea of communication. He wondered how much poor or faulty communication had to do with the absence of a connection with his wife. "It's my communication," he decided. "A major part of my disconnection with Mary is my communication." At breakfast that morning, Mary had informed him that he needed to listen more closely to his son. "What do you mean, listen to him more closely?" he had responded in surprise. "I listen to Jonathan."

Topping off his coffee, she said, "Last night, Jonathan tried to tell you about his school project, but you were too busy to listen to him."

"I heard him," Dave said defensively.

Sitting down, she smiled and said, "So, tell me about his project."

"It's a civil rights thing," he said.

Mary sat patiently, waiting for him to tell her more, but he couldn't.

She took his hand and said softly, "Jonathan is doing a paper on Martin Luther King Jr. and his influence today on African American adolescents. He is reading an overview of the paper to his class next Friday, and he asked you if you could come."

Bewildered, Dave asked, "He asked me if I could come? When?"

"While you were working on the shelves," she replied.

"What did I say?"

"You said, 'Good job. Keep up the good work. Can you hand me that screwdriver?'"

Now, sitting in his delivery truck in the parking lot, Dave thought, "How could I have been that insensitive?" He thought about his wife, daughter, and son and how much he loved them. "I am really missing the boat with communication," he realized.

Dave smiled as he thought about his family's recent trip to Disney World. He remembered Mickey Mouse and his big ears, and he came to a decision. He said to himself, "I'll ask my family for their help. When they perceive I'm not giving them my full attention, they need to ask me to put my 'big ears' on. That will be our signal that they really need me to listen. I'll try to be a good listener, but if I am failing, this is how they can help me."

9

Ownership
Meets Poser

S ince the meeting, Ownership had been reflecting on his role in the kidnapping of Excellence and what he might do to get her back. The kidnapping hit Ownership very hard. In fact, he, Excellence, and Performance were often seen together. Now that Excellence had been kidnapped and Performance had been seriously injured and was in the hospital, Ownership was feeling out of place.

Looking through some of the photographs of himself with Excellence and Performance, Ownership thought about how the three of them had each joined the organization within a short period of time. That had been several years ago, and the organization was growing well when Leadership recruited him. Ownership could recall the interview as if it was yesterday.

Leadership asked him what he considered his greatest strength.

"I help employees take full responsibility for their work," Ownership replied with pride.

"Go on," Leadership said encouragingly.

"Have you ever washed a rental car?" Ownership boldly asked.

This caught Leadership off-guard. "Well, no," was the reply.

"We don't wash rental cars because we don't own them," Ownership said. This made Leadership smile. Ownership continued, "My strength lies in helping employees reach this same understanding about their jobs—that is, how they can fully take possession of their roles and responsibilities in the organization."

"And what has your success rate been in this endeavor?" Leadership inquired.

"A very good question. A very good question indeed," Ownership answered. "I would like to say it's been 100 percent, but that would not be the truth."

Leadership was about to ask what factors led to employees' accepting Ownership and what factors prevented them from accepting him. As if reading Leadership's mind, Ownership offered, "When there is a culture of trust and inclusion, employees are more likely to accept me. However, if the organization has a history of mistrust and top-down management, I find it very difficult for the employees to accept me."

Leadership stood and walked to one of the windows in his office. Staring out, Leadership was silent for a while. Then he turned and walked back and sat down. Looking at Ownership, Leadership said, "We have worked hard here to earn the trust of our employees, and we try to include them in decisions." He added, "We really need you here."

Ownership pushed a small book across the desk to Leadership. "What's this?" Leadership asked.

With pride, Ownership replied, "It's the *Best Employee Owner's Manual*. I wrote it myself. If you will look at the table of contents, you can see the aspects of employees' jobs that I believe they should own."

Leadership turned to the table of contents and read:

Best Employee Owner's Manual

1. **Passion**—You get to choose your attitude. Choose the best!

2. **Competency**—Know what, when, and how to do it!

3. **Flexibility**—Be willing to accept new ideas and methods without compromising your values!

4. **Communication**—Listen intently and speak with clarity!

5. **Ownership**—Take charge of your actions, behavior, and performance!

It takes all of these. The whole is greater than the sum of the parts!

"This looks great!" Leadership exclaimed. "When can you start?"

Ownership proudly recalled that he joined Gorman-Scott Inc., and not long after that, Excellence came and then Performance.

Suddenly, a voice said sympathetically "Now, now."

Looking up, Ownership could make out an odd figure standing before him. "Hello," he said uncertainly. "I'm sorry. I didn't hear you come in." The person across from him could only be described as resembling a ventriloquist's dummy. He was dressed in a tuxedo, and his movements were nothing less than mechanical. Suddenly, Ownership realized that this figure actually looked like Edgar Bergen's dummy, Charlie McCarthy, but without the monocle.

"Poser is the name," the figure offered as he sat down, doffing his black top hat respectfully. Ownership was stunned when the figure froze, with raised top hat in hand and blank, staring eyes.

For a few moments, Ownership was nonplussed. Finally he hesitantly asked, "What can I do for you?"

Seemingly in response to the question, Poser returned his hat to his head and squared up in his chair. "You are asking too much of us," Poser said unequivocally. Then he froze again, mouth open, staring intently.

"Us?" Ownership asked.

Turning his head sideways, Poser replied, "Us. I represent the employees."

"I don't think I am asking too much," Ownership said tentatively. He had still not worked out who Poser really was or how he knew what Ownership was thinking.

Ownership's reply stimulated Poser into motion again. Poser smiled broadly, put one hand up as if waving, and then said, "*Your Best Employee Owner's Manual* is wishful thinking. Most employees just want to come in, do their jobs, and go home. We don't have stock in the company. We don't get recognized or rewarded for going the extra mile."

As Ownership listened to Poser, he could not help but notice Poser's eyes. They were large and unblinking and seemed to stare past him, not at him. The word that came to Ownership's mind was *vacant*. Poser's stare was vacant. Ownership had seen this exact same look on a number of employees' faces over the years. It was the look of disengagement, of being at work and going through the motions but not being connected to the work, the team members, or the company's mission. Ownership suddenly understood that sometimes the employees were, in fact, just posing.

With his hand still in a simulated wave position, Poser continued, "You—who represent the Leadership—pretend to empower us—the employees. You sit around and talk about how to get buy-in from us, how to get us to give our best, but you refuse to slow down and really listen to us, to show us the respect we want and deserve. Or what is worse," Poser said in a voice heavy with sarcasm, "is when you pretend to listen and then go ahead and do exactly what you were planning on doing in the first place. Is it any wonder that you have failed to instill a sense of ownership?" Poser cocked his head sideways, and suddenly his eyes seemed to bore right into Ownership's brain. "We are not owners. We are victims."

Then Poser opened his palms and shrugged his shoulders. "And do you know what victims do?" he said. "They do just enough to stay off the radar screen. So, then, one couldn't claim we don't do our jobs. But when a customer is knocking on the door at 7:02 p.m., and the store closed at 7, we point at the clock and mouth, 'We're closed.' And when a customer calls with an issue, we quote the policy defining the company position, but we fail to solve the customer's problem. We employees know what our specific responsibilities are, and by and large we fulfill them. But we are not being paid for helping others do their jobs or solving their problems." Poser put his hands and shoulders down, straightened his head, and again assumed that vacant, glassy-eyed look that caused Ownership to feel that Poser was looking right past him. "If you want our best, then give us your best. No empty platitudes. No excuses. No manipulation."

Ownership took a minute to compose himself and to try to fully understand Poser's comments. Finally, he said emphatically, "You may be correct about our Leadership. We have certainly learned that we must improve, but your perspective on employees is unacceptable!"

"We shall see," Poser said, getting up. "We shall see." Out of nowhere he produced a copy of the local newspaper and dropped it on Ownership's desk, and then he was gone. Ownership opened the paper and looked at the headline. It read, "Gorman-Scott Inc. Found to Be Average."

"No!" screamed Ownership. He looked down at his desk again. There was no newspaper there. Was his interaction with Poser real, or had he been dreaming?

Special Delivery: OWNERSHIP

*If you see something that needs fixin', own it,
then make it right.* —Harry Paul

It had now been some time since Excellence was kidnapped from Gorman-Scott Inc. Through Darnell, Dave kept up with the events unfolding as he made his rounds there. The kidnapping had motivated Dave to look at his own life both professionally and personally. On his way to a delivery, he thought about the areas he had been working on: passion, competency, flexibility, and communication. He truly desired to be the best in his own life. He had had a heart-to-heart with Mary, and she had forgiven him. But he knew that he had a lot of making up to do, and each day he must be on guard not to slip back into mediocrity. Philosophically, this was not a chore for him, for he truly loved Mary, but passion, competency in relationship building, flexibility, and communication did not always come naturally to him. So, day by day he had to keep a constant awareness of these areas, and he had to work at being his best.

Just then, Dave drove by a car rental shop. He chuckled as he thought about his family's last vacation. Mary had suggested that they wash the rental car before they returned it. At the time, he had thought it was ludicrous. Now he realized that Mary had an ownership mentality in everything she did. Then, suddenly, it was as if all the lessons of his life came together. "Ownership!" he exclaimed. "It's all about ownership."

That night after dinner, he sat with Mary at the kitchen table and told her about his epiphany. Deep into the discussion, he said, "So if you own it, you are more likely to take care of it."

"Quite true," she replied, noting both the simplicity and the significance of the statement.

Enthusiastically, Dave stated, "So that will be my motto: Ownership. I will take ownership of my work, my relationships—my life."

"I am behind you 100 percent," Mary said, "but no one can control all of that."

"Exactly!" Dave exclaimed. "So what I plan to do is spend my time focusing on what I can control." Remembering an old proverb he had heard, he said, "I can't direct the wind, but I can adjust my sails."

"Sounds like a good philosophy!" Mary said.

"You're right," Dave replied. "I can decide to focus on the things I can control and not become a victim of or be bitter about the things I can't. That is what being my best is about."

"You've really thought a lot about becoming your best in your life lately," she offered.

"I have," Dave admitted. "I really have. Ever since Excellence was kidnapped from one of my clients, my eyes opened, and I have been able to reach out into the future and look back at what I want my life to have represented." Barely holding back tears, he said, "And I know I want you by my side." Mary patted him on the back. She could tell how important this was to him. He said, "I want my life to have made a positive difference in others' lives. I know that sounds trite, but I really mean it."

"I know you do," she replied softly.

"I want our kids to be proud of me and the way I conduct my life." Looking at her, he said, "And I want you to be proud of me."

Hugging him, Mary said, "Dave, I don't think I could be any prouder of you."

After a few moments, he asked, "Will you help me?"

"Help you?"

"Yes, help me," he said. "In the way you have helped me before. I know myself well enough to know I can get so focused on one thing sometimes that I can't see the forest for the trees. You have always been so good at pulling me back so that I see both."

"Certainly, Dave. I plan to always be here for you."

Dave told Mary about the Dooley philosophy, and she laughed. "I want to approach every day like that," he said. "If you see me approaching life otherwise, let me know. And," he added, "I am not so naive as to not understand that bad situations happen in life. When they do, we will deal with them. But on the whole, I plan to wake up every day with renewed enthusiasm."

"That sounds good," she replied. Getting up from the table, she said, "How about you and I go for a walk? The kids have been asking me to speak to you about getting a dog. I think we should get one, and I think I know what we should name it."

10

Leadership Meets the Employees

Ownership's encounter with Poser, whether it was real or a dream, served as a wake-up call to him. He asked Leadership to bring the team together, and he shared his story with them. Interestingly, a few frontline employees were asked to be part of the meeting. When Communication questioned Leadership before the meeting about the wisdom of this move, he had replied, "Just trying to be transparent. It has become clear that Excellence has been replaced by Average, and no one even noticed until the ransom note was discovered. I believe that now our employees can more easily recognize this imposter, Average, than we can and that they are an important part of our getting our Excellence back."

The team and the frontline employees listened intently to Ownership's story. When he finished, the other members of the team related the strange interactions they too had experienced. Passion described how N. Different worked to lessen passion, energy, and enthusiasm for the work being done and the interactions taking place. Competency discussed N. Ept and how she kept people from getting the skills they needed to grow and be their best. Flexibility told about N. Flexibility—how he had people quote policy and procedure and not look for better ways or embrace change. Communication talked about Miss Communication and her unique ability to confuse the message.

When Excellence's team was done, Jenna, one of the frontline employees, said simply, "We know them all."

The entire team turned to her. "You know them all?" Communication asked, looking bewildered.

"Yes," she replied innocently, and as she did, the other employees nodded in agreement. "They are all members of the Average crew," she said.

Suddenly, Jared, another frontline employee, stood up, and the team could see that it took great courage for him to speak. "I did it," he said. "I sent the ransom note."

Excellence's team stared in amazement. Jared summoned even more courage and stated resolutely, "You see, we"—he indicated his peers—"we have known that Excellence has been missing for some time now. The employees tried to get Excellence back on our own, but after a while, we realized that it would take Leadership, Excellence's team, and us to get her back. So, I sent the ransom note to get your attention."

"Why didn't you just come and tell us?" Ownership asked.

The team didn't miss the furtive glances that the employees gave one another. Jenna spoke again. "We have tried to tell you on a number of occasions." Looking at Communication, she stated boldly, "You are pretty good at telling us what to do or what we should do and when, but sometimes you are not so good at listening."

"Please, go on," Communication said.

"Well," Jenna said, taking a deep breath, "you should understand that most of the employees want to do their best. There are only a few employees who don't pull their weight."

Jared interjected, "And they never will!"

Ownership began, "But Poser told me—"

"Excuse me for the interruption," Jared said impatiently, "but Poser does not represent us. He represents only those few employees that Jenna mentioned. Often, he's able to convince Leadership that most employees are lazy and just want to get by with the minimum. Actually, most employees want to do a really good job. We just don't always have the tools and direction we need."

Jenna smiled at Jared and then continued, "It's true. Most of us want to do our jobs well." Looking at Passion, she said, "Do you want to know what motivates us, what makes us want to strive for excellence?" Passion blushed but didn't reply. "Respect. Respect is a powerful motivator, as is caring. And we want to know that what we are doing is making a difference; recognition and appreciation are also great motivators."

Then Jenna turned to Competency. "We want to be the best at what we do. We want the right information, training, support, and technology."

She looked uncomfortably at her peers and said, "Some of us could improve our interpersonal skills and our confidence at work. Put yourself in our shoes," she said, now looking at the team. "You ask us why we don't tell you things you need to know. Well, in part, it's because you walk around with your tablet computers and your own management language, going to meetings none of us are privy to, and then you show in up in our department with some announcement of a change, and you expect the employees to start implementing it." Jenna could see that everyone on the team was listening. "Look, I am not trying to be sarcastic here. We are just asking you to help us by finding ways for us to acquire the skills we need to do our best."

Competency started squirming in her chair.

Turning now to Flexibility, Jenna said, "Most of the employees here recognize that things in our industry change very quickly, and believe it or not, we are willing to learn how to meet those challenges."

Still looking at Flexibility, she continued, "Earlier when I mentioned respect, well, this may be an opportunity to show it. It's not too much to ask us to use our own judgment and common sense. Help us understand the change, the expected outcome, and the general direction. Then, rather than giving us the absolute requirements of how to get it done, perhaps you could ask us for our opinions. You might be surprised about the ideas, thoughts, and solutions we have."

After a period of silence, Ownership added, "It seems that we all have the same goal, to get our Excellence back. Now let's start working to make this happen and raise our Performance."

"Anyone have any ideas of where we go from here?" Leadership said.

11

What Every Leader, Manager, Supervisor, and Employee Must Know About Excellence

The organization did figure out "where to go from here" and came to understand that they must strive for passion, competency, flexibility, communication, and ownership, that all five of these qualities were important in their work. Because of this, Excellence finally returned. Leadership wanted to do everything that could be done to keep Excellence front and center. And so he brought everyone together again to debrief. If there was anything they could learn from the crime of Average, Leadership wanted to share the knowledge across the organization.

Leadership had invited other Gorman-Scott Inc. leaders, managers, supervisors, and employees, and Excellence got straight to the point. Looking around the room, she smiled and then said, "First, I want to thank the employee who sent the ransom note and let Leadership know that I was missing. When I first heard about the ransom note, I somehow knew it was a way for the employees to let Leadership know there was a problem. Often, it is employees at the front line who are the first to recognize that Average has slipped in. Let me say it's good to be back. I suspect there is no one here who wants to be just average."

She paused to reconsider. "Well, there might be one or two in the organization who do just enough to get by, but for the most part we have a good group of people here." She paced for a few moments and then said, "So if most of the people here want to be their best, I want to answer two questions you may have: (1) Why did so much time go by before we realized that Excellence was missing, and (2) when we finally did recognize Average, what took us so long to get Excellence back?"

She took a few moments to allow her questions to sink in. "First off, let's admit that we're all in this together. We have people here from all different levels of the organization, and we are all culpable." People looked either surreptitiously around the room or down at the floor. "I do not say this to cast blame," Excellence continued. "I say this to encourage you to look in the mirror, not across the room.

With a wave of her hand, Excellence acknowledged her team. "You all have met Passion, Competency, Flexibility,

Communication, and Ownership," she said proudly. She turned back to the group and stated seriously, "If you want me to stay, if you want to have Excellence in your personal and professional lives, if you want to be your best, I am suggesting that you get to know them better."

Again, Excellence paced for a few moments. "So, now back to the first question of why it took so long for you to notice my absence. You didn't notice my absence because you must have *all of these* for true excellence." Excellence again gestured to Passion, Competency, Flexibility, Communication, and Ownership. "Do you remember what the ransom note said?" she asked with emotion. Holding it up, she read, "'If you ever want to see your Excellence again, open your eyes and pay the ransom.' Well, this is the ransom each organization must pay to get its own Excellence back: you must work consistently at the highest levels with Passion, Competency, Flexibility, Communication, and Ownership. And when I say 'organization,' I don't just mean those in designated positions of influence and leadership," she added authoritatively. "I mean all of you!" she said, pointing around the room. "Organizations are made up of individuals just like you, and you cannot attain organizational excellence," she said, smiling and thumping her chest, "until you have collective individual excellence.

"You see, Average's skill does not rest in promoting the substandard. It rests in nurturing mediocrity. He calls his method the Law of Average, and here is how it works: Average doesn't work to suppress Passion, Competency, Flexibility, Communication, and Ownership all at one time. He just makes sure that at least one or more of these aspects of excellence is subdued, not at its best. He knows that if he can quell just one or two of them at a time, he can keep true excellence away. And that, my friends, answers the second question of why it took so long for me to return after you realized that Average had replaced me. Attaining and keeping excellence is not for the faint of heart, nor is it a walk in the park. It takes commitment, courage, and hard work."

Excellence could tell that she had the group's attention. "Let me give you an example," she continued. "All of you know someone who is highly competent in her job. Not only is she highly competent, but also she is passionate and takes full ownership of her job. So far, so good, right? But this same person doesn't listen to others' ideas and opinions and is very rigid in the way she does things. When this person looks in the mirror, she sees herself as a team player because of her competency, passion, and ownership. The team, however, does not see the same thing because of her poor communication and inflexibility. By the Law of Average, mediocrity will ensue."

Looking around the room, Excellence added, "Or perhaps some of you know someone who is the nicest person in the world. He excels at communicating and exudes passion. He bends over backward to make situations work, and he takes full responsibility. And yet, when it comes to getting his job tasks done, he is consistently late or has mistakes in his work, and you end up doing more work or having your work slowed down because of his issue with competency. While we like to be around these people socially, when it comes to work, having four out of five of these qualities does not meet the standards of Excellence.

"So what is my message to leaders, managers, supervisors, and employees? *What is my message to you?*" Excellence inquired as she surveyed the audience. "Each of you should take an honest look in the mirror and beware the Law of Average." Smiling, she stated, "I have been asking you to take a look in the mirror. Actually, I am asking you to look deeper than that. You understand, I'm an inside-out character. Excellence," she said, pointing to herself, "starts on the inside of each individual. Once you understand and commit to my five key qualities, then your behavior begins to change. I am asking each of you to take an inventory of your actions and behavior in the areas of

- Passion

- Competency

- Flexibility

- Communication

- Ownership

"It takes practice and self-mastery in *all these areas* for you to gain and maintain Excellence in your lives." Excellence started to leave but then turned back to the group. "What I am talking about is not separate and distinct from your personal lives. This works at home too." She smiled and then said, "Don't follow the Law of Average—follow the Law of Excellence!"

THE LAW OF EXCELLENCE

Keep a constant awareness and vigilance

to always

be your best

with

Passion,

Competency,

Flexibility,

Communication, and

Ownership

Epilogue

I t was almost one year later, and Dave was again delivering a package to Gorman-Scott Inc. His route had changed shortly after Excellence returned, but he was filling in on his old route today. This organization had a special place in his heart because when Excellence disappeared, it had caused him to think deeply about his own personal and professional excellence. And what a difference that had made in his life. He walked to the administration department to see how Darnell was doing.

"I am fine!" Darnell answered. "Things are going well around here," she added, smiling.

"So how is your Passion doing?"

"Great!" she said. "Once the word got out to everyone that the frontline employees had a voice and that meaningful dialogue had begun between them and management, things changed. The employees come to work with more pride in themselves and their work. They see challenges as opportunities."

"Communication doing OK?" asked Dave.

"Oh, yes. Conversations have moved from being critical to being productive. The communication between managers, employees, and leadership is more focused, meaningful, and honest. We are getting better at having the right people address the issues in a timely manner, and guidelines are in place to ensure that everyone has a voice and important messages and information are available to all concerned. Effective listening is now an important focus of Gorman-Scott Inc."

"Improvements in Competency?"

"There certainly are," Darnell related. "The company is seeking out more educational opportunities to help employees not only with the technical aspects of their jobs but also with the interpersonal skills to improve their customer service. Employees are more interested in their personal goals and how to integrate those goals with the needs of the organization."

"What about Flexibility?"

"Oh, our Leadership was astounded by the increased openness to change from the employees. That doesn't mean there aren't questions and concerns about the changes, but there is a difference in how management handles them. It is," she paused, "well, it is being done professionally, and the questions and concerns are legitimate; some are raised that management has not seen. The employees and management are actually working as a team now. They stopped keeping score of who got what and began paying attention to what is important to the success of the organization."

"Need I even ask about Ownership?" Dave said with a grin.

Darnell was beside herself with excitement. She said, "You know, before long, most people took ownership. They abandoned the victim mentality and took more responsibility with fewer excuses. This doesn't mean that mistakes aren't made or that all is perfect. What it does mean is that everyone has stopped pointing fingers at each other for mistakes or bad outcomes, and instead they have begun to look in the mirror and ask themselves, even in the presence of barriers and constraints, what they can do to improve the outcome. And then, they constructively ask what they can do better as a team."

"And Performance?"

"Sure enough, our Performance has risen. Average and his crew are nowhere to be seen." She added, "Our sales have increased, our customer-service survey responses are getting better, our profitability is rising, and that has created more opportunity for our employees to advance. We've actually started hiring again!"

"It almost sounds too good to be true," Dave said.

Darnell blushed and then said, "Well, perhaps I have embellished a bit. We certainly still have challenges and opportunities here. It's not quite that simple or easy, but overall we are headed in the right direction."

Darnell noticed a difference in Dave, perhaps a little more pep in his step. "Enough about us," she said. "How are you doing?"

"Never better," Dave replied. Leaning in close to Darnell, he whispered, "You know, when your Excellence here was kidnapped, it had a tremendous impact on my life."

"Really?"

"Oh yes," Dave replied. "It really caused me to think about my own life, both personally and professionally."

"And?" Darnell urged.

Trying not to let his pride show too much, Dave said, "And I am up for a promotion at work. I think my boss must have recognized the changes in me. And things have never been better at home. My relationships with my wife and kids are improving."

"It affected me too," Darnell said, misty-eyed. After a few moments, she said, "This is not something I have really talked to anyone about, but my husband and I were on a path that probably would have ended in our splitting up."

"Oh, how awful!"

"Yes. I had a wake-up call, too, when our Excellence was kidnapped. Things were not going well for me at home, and I had placed most of the blame on my husband. But when I saw how the organization came together here to get back our Excellence, well, I had to question my own passion, communication, flexibility, and competency in our relationship. Once I began to take ownership of our relationship, my own behavior began to change, and, well, we still have issues, but we are together, and our relationship is getting better every day."

Dave got up and patted Darnell on the back. "Keep up the good work!"

After they said their good-byes, Dave went back to his truck. From his glove compartment, he pulled out a journal he had begun just after Excellence was kidnapped from Gorman-Scott Inc.

He read one of his favorite entries and smiled:

Make the choice each day not to be burdened by the sludge of negativity; instead, rise above it with a zest for life and desire for personal excellence.

The return of excellence to Dave's own life had truly transformed him. He closed the journal and thought about where he was going today after work. It was to the local animal shelter. Katherine and Jonathan had wanted a dog for some time, and Dave finally relented, with one stipulation. They had to name the dog Dooley. His Dooley would be a living, breathing reminder of how precious life is and how we should wake up every morning and choose to greet the day with excitement, a positive attitude, and a desire to do and be our best.

Now ELEVATE Your Excellence!

The tension between excellence and average is all too real. You start the day with passion, but after battling the same issue you thought you solved last week (and the week before), you slip into indifference. Yesterday, you were on top of your game. No one knew your job better than you. But today, the technology is more complex and the customers are more sophisticated. Competency fades to incompetency.

You have been the poster child for accepting change, but the speed and frequency of the changes are overwhelming, and your resilience has reached a limit. Your flexibility hardens into inflexibility. Communication used to be easy, fluid, and productive. But now it is discordant, and the mixed messages and ambiguity lead to routine miscommunications that drain you of your energy.

You took ownership of your job, your relationships, and your responsibilities. Over time, however, you realized that the rewards for going the extra mile were few and far between. So you could put in the minimum amount of work, time, and energy with basically the same rewards.

The problem is that this devolution happens insidiously and outside the boundaries of our awareness. Incident by incident, the thermostat of our definition of excellence gets reset. Before long, average has replaced excellence and we don't even recognize the change.

Most of us do not aspire to be average. We want to be the best—that is, excellent. Whether as mom, dad, son, brother, sister, daughter, leader, manager, supervisor, employee, Sunday school teacher, quilter, or softball player, most of us want to be the best at what we do and what we are. The problem is, average quietly creeps in, and before we know it, our excellence has been kidnapped.

There is no silver bullet for maintaining excellence, but we believe that attention to the core principles put forth in *Who Kidnapped Excellence?* can help you to cultivate awareness and pour a foundation that will keep you moving toward a higher level of excellence. We offer the following model to ELEVATE to your best:

Examine Yourself

Live Like Dooley

Equip Yourself

Verify and Clarify

Accept Change

Take Responsibilty

Expect Improved Performance

Examine Yourself

Now it's time for a reality check! Has your excellence been kidnapped? When you look at the aspects of your personal and work life, what is the pattern of your passion, competency, communication, flexibility, and ownership? In fact, to bring the abstract closer to reality, choose the area of your life (manager, employee, spouse, parent, etc.) you think you could improve the most, and rate yourself on the following items, with 1 being never and 10 being always:

	Never Always
My attitude is great	1 2 3 4 5 6 7 8 9 10
I look at opportunities with enthusiasm	1 2 3 4 5 6 7 8 9 10
My life is a journey of learning and discovery	1 2 3 4 5 6 7 8 9 10
I learn something new every day	1 2 3 4 5 6 7 8 9 10
I actively listen before responding	1 2 3 4 5 6 7 8 9 10
I look at change as "What I am gaining, not losing?"	1 2 3 4 5 6 7 8 9 10
I am accepting of new ideas	1 2 3 4 5 6 7 8 9 10
If I see it, I own it and I fix it	1 2 3 4 5 6 7 8 9 10
I act like an owner and take pride in what I am doing	1 2 3 4 5 6 7 8 9 10
I do my best every day	1 2 3 4 5 6 7 8 9 10

How did you do?

Now it's time for the *real* reality check. Choose a person who is part of the area of your life in which you selected to rate yourself, and ask him or her to rate you as well! This inventory check will help you to better understand yourself.

Dave took the survey and was fairly pleased with the outcome. But when his wife, at his request, rated him, he had to take a step back. He had begun keeping a journal that he had simply named "My Best!" After the survey, he wrote:

> My Best! There is quite a gap between the ratings.
> I rated myself higher on most items than Mary did.
> I need to learn more about why there is this differ-
> ence. Tonight I will sit down with her and ask her
> to tell me more. I must be on guard so that I don't
> become defensive. If I am really striving for excel-
> lence, I must value input like this.

Other excerpts from Dave's journal falling under the category of *Examine Thyself* include:

- Identified the "next person(s) in the process" in the important areas of my life (my spouse, my children, and my boss).

- I have a great relationship with my supervisor. Asked him to list two areas where I could improve my performance. He seemed impressed that I asked.

- Asked my family to list two areas where I could improve our relationship. It is clear that I need to be a better listener and should keep an open mind!

- Reviewed the last six months and listed items I completed successfully. After I finished reviewing the list, I learned some things I am doing well and also some areas where I could improve.

- Asked colleagues to describe to me one way in which I could help them. Recorded the ways I have fulfilled their requests. At the end of six weeks, I went to them and reviewed the list. They gave me feedback about what was most helpful.

Live Like Dooley! (Passion)
Inspires everyone with energy, enthusiasm, and caring.

Passion's job is to create that zest for life that causes us to smile even when circumstances are against us, to go that extra mile, and to see our life and work as an opportunity, not something we have to get through.

Develop a habit of approaching each day with a great attitude. Whatever door you need to go through, do it like Dooley, like it's the first time you've ever been through that door, like you can't wait to go out and explore.

We are not talking about a pie-in-the-sky or Pollyanna mentality that ignores the realities of life. We are talking about your ability to make a choice to see each day, situation, or challenge with fresh eyes. We are talking about your ability to make the choice each day not to be burdened by the sludge of negativity—instead, to rise above it with a zest for life and a desire for personal excellence. Dave was particularly fond of this mantra. Here are some specific actions he took to Live Like Dooley:

From "My Best!":

- Listed the items (projects) I had going on in my life. Examined them and listed the best possible outcome for each item. Then determined what steps I needed to take to get the result I desired. I made a commitment to always be ready to race out the door like Dooley.

- Realized that challenges (problems) often make me a better person. Have thought through the issues I was facing with a clear perspective of the problem, which drove me to an outcome I had not yet considered.

- Evaluated how I interact with the people around me. Dooley, like most dogs, has never missed an opportunity to greet someone enthusiastically. I will do the same.

- Have been thinking about the people who work with me and have been evaluating my social interactions with them. Playing on a team will motivate me to get out the door in the morning. Working to make others succeed is a surefire way to increase my own success.

- My environment has a tremendous impact on my attitude. When I find myself in a hostile or negative environment, I will simply remove myself from the situation. I know that criticism is contagious, and if I stay around it long enough, I will catch it.

- Someone once told me that positive actions are like buckets that are never emptied. I can pass out compliments, offer smiles, and encourage others, and the bucket will never go dry. I commit to positive actions.

- Will accept my circumstances. All the complaining in the world will not fix my situation. I will spend my time developing a strategy to overcome issues and offer solutions to those around me. My attitude will be contagious, and when others catch what I have, they will want to see the world like Dooley!

Equip Yourself (Competency)

Ensures that everyone has all the skills needed to do their best.

Competency is not just important in the technical aspects of our work and lives but also important in our relationships with one another.

Whether it is in your personal life or your professional life, competency is required for excellence. Make sure that you have the tools to deliver excellence. If you desire to be a better parent, find the resources to help with those skills. If you desire to be an excellent employee, find a manager or mentor to guide you.

Also, do not discount the competency needed in interpersonal skills to reach excellence. You may be the smartest person in the room with the highest level of technical skills, but if you do not possess the interpersonal skills that help you relate to people, you will not reach your potential. Seek out the right resources to coach yourself in this area.

Dave had several items in his journal under the category of *Equip Yourself*.

From "My Best!":

- Found a mentor! Although I have thought of mentors as being older, I found that age is not as important as skill development. My mentor challenged me to grow in some specific areas of my life. We meet once a week, and his advice has been invaluable to me.

- Started keeping a notebook where I record items about the people I meet, so that I can refresh my memory when I meet them again. It takes time and energy to journal this information, but it has already proved valuable. The surprise on people's faces when I ask about a Little League game, upcoming marriage, or job promotion encourages me to keep up my efforts in this endeavor.

- Asked my supervisor to choose a conference or training opportunity for me in an area where she would like to see me succeed. What supervisor would not want to see someone try to improve?

- Have set measurable and specific goals. I started with "I am going to be a better husband to my Mary." But my mentor asked me, how would I know if I was actually accomplishing this? I answered, "By hearing my wife say how much she appreciates me for the little things I do. Like sending flowers on her birthday and our anniversary, having coffee with her twice a week before work, and greeting her with a smile every morning."

- Have learned to laugh at my own mistakes. That doesn't mean that I am not learning from them.

- I am taking my personal and professional performance seriously, but I am taking myself a little less seriously!

Verify and Clarify (Communication)

Clearly communicates roles and expectations.

Perception is everything, and perception is created by Communication. Communication respects that there is a delicate balance between listening and talking.

The road to excellence is a two-way street paved with communication. It involves active listening and the clear articulation of our thoughts and ideas.

Here is what Dave did to improve in the area of *Verify and Clarify*.

From "My Best!":

- Now I close my computer and put away my cell phone and other potential distractions when I am speaking and listening.

- Try to listen to (the words and the tone of) what the other person is saying.

- Watch for body language and other visible signs from the other person.

- When my message is complex, I write it down before I give it. Next, I say it aloud to myself and/or I find a neutral party to try it on. Have begun to verify that I have heard the accurate message by using phrases such as, "This is what I think I heard you say." Then I say what I thought I heard them say and ask, "Is that correct?" I will need to use some judgment here. I must alter my language to fit my personality, so that it does not come across as contrived or mechanical. I try to find a way to ensure that the message is received as I intended.

- I am the one responsible for ensuring that communication has been effective. I will ask if I need to clarify any points to make them crystal clear.

- When communication derails, I will take the time to understand what I can do to improve the next time. I will identify who the next person in the process is when this happens. Perhaps I will have either a teaching moment or an "Aha!" learning moment on my hands.

Accept Change (Flexibility)

*Helps us respond to unique situations
whenever they occur.*

The only thing that remains constant is that everything changes. Flexibility understands this and helps employees to deal with and manage changes in a practical and professional manner.

The bumper sticker reads, "CHANGE IS EASY. YOU GO FIRST!" The irony here is that change is not easy, but you must "go first." You must do your best to understand the change, determine your role, and begin moving forward. Sometimes you're the one initiating the change, and sometimes you're the one who is being asked to change. We do not suggest that you accept change without questioning or seeking input, but we do suggest that flexibility—your ability to manage your response in a mature, reasonable, and professional manner—is a basic tenet of excellence in your personal and professional life.

Being flexible in times of change was difficult for Dave. The following was what he did to *Accept Change*.

From "My Best!":

- Will start by giving the people who are leading the change the benefit of the doubt and assume that the change was thought through. I must remember that I may go through a range of emotions when there are changes. My questions are, what it is, why now, and how will it affect me? All of these are normal.

- Will resist unfairly condemning a new practice before I hear all of the details of the change.

- When a change is occurring, I will develop a personal plan of action to implement it, and I will write it down.

- Will make a list of change items I have initiated over the past year and evaluate the list carefully.

- Will remember that the ability to initiate and accept change is something that can set me apart from everyone else.

- Will remember that I have more leverage when I do want to question a change if I am not someone who always resists changes.

- Will involve others around me when I work through a change process. The more I involve others, the more ownership they will have.

Take Responsibility (Ownership)

Ensures that everyone takes 100 percent responsibility for their job.

Ownership is a personal value that mirrors the knowledge that we have power and influence when we accept our responsibilities. Even in the face of constraints and barriers, we have the choice to operate using our judgment.

See it. Own it. Fix it. Improve it!

Dave realized the importance of an owner's mentality, and he did the following to *Take Ownership*.

From "My Best!":

- Will tell my close friends, spouse, and coworkers what I have learned about myself and ask them to help me with the changes in attitudes and behaviors I have committed to. Even owners need mentors and coaches.

- When that inner voice is creating a dialogue about the right thing to do, I will simply ask and answer the question, "What would I do if I owned it?"

- Will focus my energy on what I can do to positively affect the outcome of the situations or the challenges I am confronted with. Owners do not pass the buck!

- Will practice joint ownership. Many challenges and opportunities are best solved and seized by a collective group. I will take ownership seriously, but I won't be selfish with it when a team approach is needed.

- Will practice preventive maintenance.

- Will be a producer and guard against the entitlement mind-set.

- Will stop myself before I say the word "they" and determine if what I am about to say is productive.

- Will go to meetings prepared. Whenever possible, I will get the agenda and objectives of the meeting in advance and come prepared to add value.

- Will maintain a keen awareness of my goals (personal and professional). And I will keep score. Then I will know where I am in relationship to the goal. If I get off track, I will get focused and/or get help!

- Whether or not it's my responsibility, if I can make something right, I will do it!

- Will assume that someone is watching me in everything I do—because someone is!

Expect Improved Performance

In *The 7 Habits of Highly Effective People*, author Stephen Covey talks about things being created twice, first in the mind and then in reality. And so it is true with excellence—excellence does not just show up on your doorstep and ask to come in! Excellence begins to show up in your life and in your work, first, with a mind-set change, and second, with the repeated practice of those behaviors that are consistent with the mind-set.

Early in the book, we stated that the characters of Performance and Excellence were often seen together. In reality, performance is improved when you elevate your excellence. Thus, excellent performance is an outcome of a high level of passion, competency, flexibility, communication, and ownership. Similarly, average performance is an outcome of mediocrity and results when you do not have high levels in *all* these categories consistently. As you elevate your excellence, people (your boss, your spouse, your peers, your employees, your kids, and most important, you) will begin to notice the improvement in your performance.

Unless people are or have been in therapy, they generally are uncomfortable talking about their behavior. And yet, how we behave toward one another in our relationships at home and at work is foundational to the achievement of excellence. Passion, competency, flexibility, communication, and ownership all begin with a mind-set that is manifested in the behaviors we choose.

So, what is stopping you from your choosing to take the next step toward excellence? And, for the most part, it *is* a choice. We recognize that at different times in our lives, we all experience unique circumstances (a death, a health issue, a significant loss, etc.), but, notwithstanding one of these major events, we all have a choice about our passion, our competency, our flexibility, our communication, and our ownership mentality.

Do not accept average in your life! Begin your journey to ELEVATE your Excellence!

People and Companies Who 'Get It'

*Customer-service excellence—if the company
doesn't get it, the customers won't get it,
either. —John Britt*

Excellence is a journey, not a destination. The authors
have had personal experience with the following people
and companies, who, in our opinion, get it. While all of
them have attained excellence, and the five traits are
present, we chose to highlight just a few for the sake of
efficiency.

We trust the following examples will inspire you to
give and be your best.

Jack, the Coffee Tastes Better
When You Make It!

Jack was in a local delicatessen in Philadelphia on a chilly fall day having brunch with Sarah, his wife of sixty-three years. As they were enjoying each other's company, Jack noticed a young man approaching their table. As it turned out, he was a customer at the Wawa convenience store, where Jack worked the coffee counter three mornings a week. The young man greeted Jack and told him that he had dropped in to the Wawa that morning for a cup of coffee, and it didn't taste nearly as good as it did when Jack was there making it. Jack smiled and thanked the young man for being a regular Wawa customer and for stopping by their table with his kind words. He then turned to his wife and said with a laugh, "Sarah, nice man, but how could the coffee taste better when I make it? It's Wawa brand coffee, and it is supplied in premeasured pouches; the water comes out of a filtered tap directly into the coffee machine. And all coffee pots hold the same amount. How could it possibly taste better when I make it?" Jack thought for a moment and said to his wife, "I think I know why it tastes better when I make it, Sarah—it's because I rinse out the coffee pots really well each time before I brew a new pot. That has to be it—I rinse the pots out well. That's why the coffee tastes better." Sarah smiled and said, "Yes, Jack, I'm sure that's the reason."

But who's Jack? Actually, Jack was my (Harry Paul's) father. He lived in the northeast section of Philadelphia, was eighty-seven years young at the time of his passing, and had worked part-time at a Wawa. He was the oldest employee at Wawa, a family-owned chain of almost four hundred convenience stores located throughout the mid-Atlantic states. He worked the coffee counter three mornings a week at a store located just a few miles from his home. Jack absolutely loved his customers—he loved talking to them, sharing stories with them, and getting to know them. He shared himself with them, and they in turn shared themselves with him. In a manner of speaking, he was the mayor of Wawa.

When my dad told me the story about the man at the delicatessen saying how the coffee tasted better when he made it, and said that he thought it was because he washed out the pots so well, I started to laugh. When I asked him if he really thought this was the reason, he said, "Sure, what else can it be?" I said it wasn't that the pots were cleaner. Well-washed pots are a given. I said, "Dad, you make the coffee taste better." Jack answered with some doubt in his voice, "I do?" At this point I said, "Sure, you do. It's because you like people, you're nice to them, and you're interested in them. You share yourself with them, make them laugh, and create a positive experience for them, and in turn they share some of themselves with you, all of it making the coffee seem to taste better. You're helping them start their day off on an upbeat note, and I'm sure they really appreciate it, besides the better-tasting coffee. You do naturally what organizations strive to do to attain and maintain success; you're creating a positive experience for your customers. You're making a big-time difference in their lives."

Jack was the sweetener in the coffee, the missing element that people are hungry for in this fast-paced, technology-driven world we live in. Look at what you are doing and find the missing ingredients, the ones that cause you to look forward to going to work and making a difference for people. Everyone can make a difference, just like Jack.

Jack's behavior did not go unnoticed by Wawa's management. They awarded him with a gold medal for outstanding customer service—three years in a row! After receiving his third medal, he said to me with a smile. "I still think it's because the pots are cleaner." I responded, laughing, "Dad, they may be cleaner, but remember, you make the coffee taste better."

Not long after that, Wawa built another store closer to Jack's house. Transferring to the new store gave him a shorter commute time; when you are eighty-six years old, seconds count. Jack did not go alone to the new store. Scores of his customers followed him to the new store, and it wasn't because he rinsed the pots better. The new store's coffee business was brisk and growing. People looked forward to coming into Wawa every morning that Jack was working, for his great attitude, warm smile, friendly conversation, and great-tasting coffee.

Excellence!
Jack Paul got it, and so did his customers!

On a freezing-cold January day in 2009, Jack was laid to rest with military honors. When I got up to deliver my eulogy, I looked over the folks crowded into the funeral home and was awestruck by how many people were there—many of whom I didn't know. I did not speak of Jack's being a devoted husband, father, grandfather, and friend, or the fact that he was twice decorated for bravery as a World War II paratrooper—I assumed that most already knew this. Instead, I spoke about how Jack taught us that we all could make someone's life a little brighter, and I shared with them the story of how he had made the coffee taste better. Afterward, many people came up to me, including his fellow employees, customers, and caregivers who felt compelled to be there because Jack had made such a difference in their lives. Not only did he bring some joy to them, but he also gave them a fresh perspective on how precious life is and that we all have the ability and responsibility to make another person's life a little brighter. For many months after Jack's passing, my mom continued to receive cards, letters, and notes from his customers telling her how much they had enjoyed seeing and spending time with my dad whenever he was working at Wawa.

It's the little things you do for customers that count the most. It doesn't take much to brighten someone's day and make him or her feel great, but such actions have a huge impact on the success of the company. The good news is that doing the things that create exceptional customer experiences does not cost the company a dime. On the other hand, the impact of these simple but caring actions can have a huge effect on the company's bottom line in terms of increased productivity, market share, and profitability. This is what all companies want to see much more of and what companies must have to thrive.

Baptist Hospital

A twenty-year-old young man awoke one morning with life-threatening symptoms. This was every parent's nightmare. On the previous evening, his parents had taken him to a local immediate-care facility, and he had been diagnosed with simple bronchitis, but today, his symptoms painted a picture of a much more severe problem. His parents rushed him to Baptist Hospital, and the following excerpts from a letter they ultimately wrote tell the story of excellence in patient care.

"From the minute we stepped into the hospital, our son was treated with respect and compassion. The triage nurse immediately recognized his critical status and quickly ushered us into a treatment room. I do not remember her name, but I cannot thank her enough for being so quick to recognize his symptoms and knowing that he needed to be seen stat. She was the first of many pieces that fell into place so that our son would live. In the ER, the doctor took over the care. What a wonderfully talented physician he is! We will forever be grateful for his expertise in diagnosing potential bacterial meningitis and starting treatment. Within minutes he had stabilized our son, started testing, and discussed his diagnosis with two very scared and numb parents. The doctor realized that he was not only treating our son, he was helping us understand what was happening. He is certainly a credit to your hospital and to his profession! Believing that our child did indeed have bacterial meningitis, he quickly called in a specialist, and our son was placed into his capable and compassionate hands. I remember looking at his warm eyes hidden behind a mask that morning and feeling uncertain yet confident that whatever needed to be done would be. He began an aggressive plan to save our son. The team selflessly dedicated many, many hours to our son's care, and it is because of those long hours that he is still with us.

"Immediately after leaving the ER that morning, our son was taken to the Coronary Care Unit. All we can say is, what an incredibly dedicated team of nurses and assistants! Every single person on that floor demonstrated such a commitment to our son that went far beyond what we could have expected. As parents, we were amazed at the care each nurse and assistant took. They hugged us and reassured us that everything that could be done was. In all the chaos they offered a sweet smile and a warm hug every time we visited. We always knew that our son was in very loving and capable hands. We were constantly amazed at the endless work that was involved in his care. We sometimes felt a little overwhelmed with the medicines, the machines, the medical terms, but oh how wonderful it was the first morning we came in and saw that an assistant had bathed and shaved our son. She took such gentle care of him and we were very touched. Incidences like that happened over and over again the entire time he was in CCU. Those nurses never stopped from the minute they arrived through the doors of the unit until they left at the shift change. To say we love and respect them is so inadequate. The day our son left CCU the nurses all gathered in the hallway giving hugs and best wishes for his continued recovery. They were celebrating him, but they should also celebrate a job well done. Whatever salary they receive can never be enough for what they give to each patient that comes through their unit.

"After leaving CCU, our son continued his recovery in the Palliative Care unit due to an overflow of patients. He again received outstanding care from a wonderful staff. It was easy to see that they are committed to excellent care for all patients. They took a personal interest in his recovery and pampered him beyond words!

"The Baptist Hospital family, from the x-ray techs to food service staff to janitorial staff, treated us superbly. We can't tell you how many staff persons stopped to ask about our son and to tell us they were continuously praying for our family. It was easy to see that the people who work at your hospital truly feel a sense of family . . . and coming from parents who lived through a horrendous experience, that "family" meant the world! Our prayer is that they will never underestimate what influence they have on families who come to your hospital. They each played such an important role in our son's recovery.

"In closing, we would like to again extend our most sincere gratitude for everything that was done for our son and our family. Baptist Hospital demonstrated what health care should always be about! Truthfully, the afternoon our son was released and we pulled out of the parking lot, we both had tears in our eyes. We knew just how different an outcome we could have had if not for the diligent and compassionate team at Baptist Hospital."

Company: Baptist Hospital

Founded: 1975

Located: Louisville, Kentucky

Profile: Baptist Hospital, a 519-bed community acute-care hospital with fifty-seven thousand annual emergency room visits and thirty thousand admissions, is a leading health-care provider in the Louisville metropolitan area. With a workforce of more than four thousand, it is one of Louisville's top-ten private-sector employers.

Excellence in customer service is rooted in the values of Baptist Hospital. Originating from this heritage are the values of respect, integrity, collaboration, excellence, and stewardship. It is therefore expected that the operations of the organization will be accomplished in accordance with these ethical values and the deep commitment of Baptist Hospital to its customers. These values guided the selection of a framework for customer service.

Excellence!
The people at Baptist Hospital get it, and so do their customers!

This is just one of the many stories of excellence at Baptist Hospital. The competency of the health-care providers stands out in this letter from two very grateful parents. The passion that the employees have for their jobs almost jumps off the pages, and the hospital's commitment to communication is phenomenal. Health care is a complicated business, and the excellence in patient care did not happen in just one department. It happened in the emergency room, the coronary care unit, the medical surgical unit, and all of the ancillary departments. Even the hospital's wellness center, Milestones, consistently is recognized as "the best place to work out" in Louisville, Kentucky. Customers do not look at their experiences from a departmental perspective; they just see and feel the experience. If one employee or one department fails in its mission for excellence, the experience backslides into average or worse.

First Choice Home Medical

"Your company saved my life!" That's what the woman in the wheelchair said to Skip Wirth when he asked how he could help his customer. Intrigued by this wonderful sentiment, he responded, "I am glad we did, but just how did we save your life?" She replied that years earlier, she had been involved in an accident that rendered her partially paralyzed and required her to be in a wheelchair. She recalled that while she was still in the hospital, she was basically told, "Go home and live your life." The problem was, nobody explained how to go home and live her life. "I was totally unprepared for the challenges to come," she said.

She went on to relate, "Buying medical equipment is not like buying a used car. You don't go in, find something, and think, that's pretty, I want that. You find what is best for you. Unfortunately, some companies just say, 'Whatever you want.' Well, that's not the case; it is what you need that is best. From the time I entered the store and met the office staff, from the technicians to the people behind the business, they obviously cared about what I needed. Not what I wanted, not what I thought was nice. They cared about what was important for me. It took a while, but they saw to it that I got what was the right chair for my problems."

Did the staff at First Choice Home Medical really save her life? Not in the sense of actually rescuing her from death, but absolutely in terms of improving the quality of her life. Because they made positioning adjustments to her wheelchair and educated her on simple home modifications, she was able to resume her busy life as a schoolteacher.

Company: First Choice Home Medical

Founded: 2003

Located: Bowling Green, Kentucky

Profile: First Choice Home Medical is a durable medical equipment (DME) company that provides home medical equipment to patients in South Central Kentucky. Their thirteen health-care professionals have over 175 years of combined health-care experience, and their care, compassion, and commitment are evident in every service they provide.

Excellence in customer service is at the heart of First Choice Home Medical. It is at the core of everything they do. Their mission statement summarizes their values:

> First Choice Home Medical is committed to the customer's right to choose. Our choice is to make a difference by providing our customers with quality equipment, service, and compassion.

Their commitment to excellence in customer service is at the forefront of their thinking. The team listens to what the patients are telling them. The team also listens to what their referral sources are telling them, and that information has been invaluable. Throughout the years, their patient and referral-source satisfaction surveys have been most gratifying.

Thad Connally III, president and owner of First Choice Home Medical, states, "Our business approach is all about quality. If we don't have quality, then we just don't have anything. We want to make sure that when you call, you understand that we will be there in a timely fashion." It has always been his desire to own his own business and his passion to take care of others. He believes that First Choice Home Medical has made significant contributions to Bowling Green and South Central Kentucky. That is a view shared by many others. In 2010, Thad was honored as the Small Business Person of the Year in Bowling Green, Kentucky.

Long before First Choice Home Medical opened, Thad and Skip used to wax philosophically about what a great company would look like. They would have a company built on trust and accountability. The team would be focused on care, compassion, commitment, integrity, and an ownership of the company's mission. Their favorite mantra was, "Bigger is not better; better is better." Their goal was never to be the biggest DME company, only to be the best. That message is communicated at every staff meeting—"We are in the business of caring."

How this mind-set is accomplished begins before a staff member is hired. The expectations of every team member are clearly communicated during the interview process, orientation, staff meetings, and annual performance appraisals. Their staff meetings are never dull because every team member is not only encouraged but expected to contribute. Because they trust one another, each member is empowered to offer new ideas, suggestions for improvement, success stories, or requests for assistance. That trust also lends itself to their holding one another accountable. Quite simply, they are very intolerant of service failures.

Excellence!
The people at First Choice Home Medical
get it, and so do their customers!

Because of the highly regulated nature of the DME business, companies do not compete on price. In essence, the price, per se, is defined by the payer sources, and thus the major competitive factor becomes service. The story of the woman who felt as if First Choice Home Medical had saved her life is one of many that demonstrate the company's passion—the kind of passion it takes to earn patients' business. They have a highly competent team whose members can deliver not only the complex technical aspects of their service but also the skills that are interpreted by the patient as caring. Their communication is transparent, and the team consistently demonstrates flexibility. Clear direction from the leadership has resulted in the ownership experienced by all employees who do their jobs as if they own the company!

Southwest Airlines

In an industry long plagued by rising costs, poor customer service, dissatisfied workers, bankruptcies, and revolving-door leadership, one airline stands contrary to this pattern. Southwest Airlines has long enjoyed success and a dedicated customer following. They have enjoyed over forty years of profitability, stable leadership, and some of the industry's highest customer-service scores. There is a reason why Southwest is called the LUV airline. It is central to who they are.

Here is just one story that represents Southwest's unique customer service:

"She made me feel like I was the only passenger on the plane!" The attendant thought Katie looked scared and weak, and so she gave her a hug and told her that everything was going to be all right. And that was exactly what Katie needed right then, because Katie was 2000 miles from home as she boarded the Southwest Airlines flight that would take her to the city where she would have open-heart surgery. And the attendant didn't stop there. She found the hospital where Katie was having surgery and called to make sure that everything, in fact, was all right. Katie survived the surgery and will never forget the friendly face that emerged in a sea of strangers and gave her hope and comfort.

Company: Southwest Airlines

Founded: 1967

Located: Dallas, Texas

Profile: Southwest Airlines is the largest carrier in the United States, based upon originating domestic passengers carried. Along with subsidiary Air Tran, it has forty-five thousand employees, operates more than thirty-seven hundred flights per day, and operates scheduled service to ninety-seven destinations in forty-one states.

Excellence!
The people at Southwest Airlines get it, and so do their customers!

Part of Southwest Airlines' success revolves around their philosophy of hiring people with the right attitude (passion) and potential. While competency is an obvious requirement for such a regulated industry, they don't stop at how they do their jobs but continue with why and how to make flying a fun and engaging experience. The company places value on people being themselves (flexibility) at work. It is not unusual to see the pilot help clean the plane when a quick turnaround is required.

Southwest Airlines is perhaps best at recognizing the next person in the process as their customer, and that begins with their employees. The employees will tell you that because the company treats them with respect, it is easy to treat the passengers with respect, and thus the employees take ownership of their duties. Not only do they take ownership of their duties—they also come together as a team when the pressure is on. They have put who they are out there in reality television shows that showcase what goes on day in and day out at Southwest

Airlines. Communication is paramount in keeping planes flying and on time. It is also important between passengers and flight crews, ground crews, and ticket and gate agents. When a challenge arises, team members spring into action and solve it, usually right on the spot. Their communications are innovative in the way they convey safety greetings and announcements. You can see many examples of Southwest's innovative communications on YouTube.

Employees say, "We are like family here. We have fun, and we love our jobs. Everybody counts and everybody cares." One employee said it this way: "We have hearts on our planes, and there is a reason for that."

Mitchells Family of Stores

The extraordinary vision of Mitchells | Richards | Marshs is to "hug" the customer—to enhance and add value to the retail experience. They are obsessed with extraordinary customer service and creating a uniquely warm environment, because anyone who becomes a customer has an enduring relationship with Mitchells | Richards | Marshs. Their motto is "Once a customer, always a friend." They give back to their communities and build trusting relationships with customers and friends that will last throughout generations. That is exactly what Mitchells | Richards | Marshs does to maintain their excellence.

Company: Mitchells | Richards | Marshs

Founded: 1958

Located: Westport, Connecticut

Profile: One of the most successful high-end luxury retail groups of stores in the world, offering men's and women's clothes, jewelry, and accessories. Located in five cities on both coasts, the stores comprise over one hundred thousand square feet of retail space. They're not successful because they have better products or prices than their competition; it's because of how they treat their customers. Mitchells is still independent, family owned, and operated by a second and third generation of Mitchells who are looking forward to serving their customers for many generations to come.

They do this with passion and grab each customer with warmth as he or she crosses the threshold at all of their stores. They know their top one thousand customers very well. Why? Because they care and know that the customers are important. And it's not just the customers that Mitchells I Richards I Marshs cares about but also the customers' children, as each store has a kids' corner. Since the first Mitchells store opened in 1958, a pot of coffee is always on; now that includes lattes and cappuccinos. Everyone concentrates on the customer and knows that they are interdependent with the customer experience. The competency that everyone has takes them beyond having product knowledge to being productive and important members of the team and creating unique and memorable customer experiences. Designers and manufacturers spend time each season to make sure that the staff members at all the stores are familiar with the latest fashions, jewelry, and accessories.

They use the collective ingenuity of three generations of Mitchells to ensure this ongoing learning culture. Everyone, from the family and management to all team members, understands that change is part of success, and all are flexible at adapting to an ever-changing environment. Execution is everything, whether it is a new fashion trend or the change in how people are dressing for success. Communication is key to their success in ensuring a seamless, outstanding customer experience no matter which of their stores you visit. Everyone at Mitchells I Richards I Marshs has ownership of every aspect of the customer experience, from the parking attendants and salespeople to the cashiers and tailors.

Excellence!
The people at Mitchells | Richards | Marshs get it, and so do their customers!

Mitchells | Richards | Marshs is successful not because they recognize the importance of customer relationships but because they make them happen.

Galt House Hotel

What do the managers of a standard hotel do when they are told that approximately one thousand visually impaired people, many of whom are bringing service animals, would like to hold a weeklong convention on the property? At the very best, panic! At the very worst, turn down the reservation. Most standard hotels do not have the facilities, funds, or willingness that it takes to host such a conference. Fortunately, Galt House Hotel is far from standard, with a drive for excellence in customer service that is second to none in the hospitality industry.

Company: Galt House Hotel

Founded: 1972

Located: Louisville, Kentucky

Profile: Founded by Al J. Schneider, Galt House Hotel boasts 1,290 guest rooms, including 650 suites. The hotel has fifty-three meeting rooms, two beautiful ballrooms, and six restaurants onsite. Stated simply, the Al J. Schneider Company, parent company of Galt House Hotel, cares. In 1969, when downtown Louisville was in decline and the riverfront was deserted, Mr. Schneider cared. He cared because he was a builder with a vision who was not afraid of working hard and taking risks. Louisville was his town, his home, and the people of Louisville were his extended family. Mr. Schneider invested his time, money, energy, and expertise in rebuilding his home, downtown Louisville. In 1972, he built a hotel. When Mr. Schneider retired, he handed the reins over to his daughter, Mary Mosely, who shared his love of Louisville and carried on the vision for the hotel.

From July 6 through 14, 2012, the American Council of the Blind held their 51st Annual Conference and Convention at Galt House Hotel, and the hotel staff and management pulled out all the stops (flexibility). All the stairs in the hotel were highlighted with reflective tape so that partially sighted guests could better see them. All hotel signage and restaurant menus were imprinted with lettering that was in braille or enlarged for better viewing. Room keycards were marked with raised labels for ease of use by the visually impaired. Hotel employees of all levels happily assisted the convention guests and guided them to different parts of the hotel (passion), not because the employees were directly instructed to do so but because it just came naturally to them. Galt House Hotel even constructed four sheltered dog walk areas for the personal needs of companion animals and scheduled a thorough, deep cleaning of the entire hotel grounds for the week after the conference departure.

Janet Dickelman, of the American Council of the Blind, said afterward in a card to the hotel,

"[Galt House Hotel] staff went above and beyond the call of duty. The housekeeping staff was careful not to move personal items in the rooms and helped frequently to find misplaced items. Everyone from the bellboys to the management was physically helping to guide our attendees from point to point in the hotel, and we appreciated that so much."

The staff at Galt House Hotel demonstrated their competency and took ownership in circumstances requiring flexibility to meet the needs of a unique customer. This is just one example of how the employees strive for excellence.

Excellence!
The people at Galt House Hotel get it,
and so do their customers!

Acknowledgments

We are very grateful to have such a supportive team helping us with the realization of *Who Kidnapped Excellence?* We are fortunate to have found a fine home for the book at Berrett-Koehler Publishing and want to especially single out and recognize Steve Piersanti, the president of Berrett-Koehler and our editor, for seeing the potential of this project and helping us to achieve the dream of publishing this book. The whole team at Berrett-Koehler has embraced this project with zest, enthusiasm, and creativity to help shape it and spread the word about *being your best*. A special shout-out goes to Jeevan Sivasubramaniam.

Thanks to Cindy Britt, whose editing expertise helped us to hone the message of this book; to Mary Paul, who gave us suggestions that made sure people understood more easily what we were saying; and to Patricia Jent, for countless readings and suggestions for the manuscript.

As authors, we believe the market should help shape the message of our book. We are fortunate to have such a supportive network of friends and colleagues who helped with their ideas and suggestions and read countless drafts to refine the manuscript and message. You are too numerous to mention, but know that you are greatly appreciated by us and that people who read this book will benefit from your wisdom.

We would like to acknowledge some great mentors who have demonstrated excellence: Gerald Embry, Ronald Jent, Pete Walters, Woody Hunt, Gene Reynolds, Joe Trybone, Gene Ference, Ray Newcomb, Greg Shelton, Ross Reck, Kevin Ezell, Tim Nobles, Randy White, and Tom James. Thanks for making it fun to strive for excellence together!

And last but not least, we want to thank Richard Andrews, friend and colleague, who acted and continues to act as our guide and mentor to help share the message of excellence and being your best with the world.

About the Authors

Harry Paul

For over thirty years, Harry Paul's career has been about helping people and organizations to be their best. His writing, speaking, and training showcase common threads throughout his work: having fun at what you are doing at work, no matter what it is you do; helping people to

be their best at work and at home; and showing organizations how to keep their employees fully engaged. Harry's latest book, *Who Kidnapped Excellence?*, expertly weaves these threads together to help people and organizations strive for excellence.

Harry developed the first thread of having fun at work while he was a senior vice president at the Ken Blanchard Companies. That's where he coauthored his first book, *FISH! A Proven Way to Boost Morale and Improve Results. FISH!* was on various best-seller lists for over six years straight and is one of the best-selling business books of all time. As a result of this success, Harry travels the world sharing the philosophy with audiences.

The second thread is helping people to be their best; it led to several more best-selling books, including *REVVED!*, coauthored with Dr. Ross Reck, which helps managers and leaders to understand the importance of recognizing and appreciating people when they go the extra mile—building an Army of Advocates who can't wait to work hard for you.

The third thread keeps people engaged—a challenge faced by many companies worldwide, especially in these tough economic times, because full employee engagement can be as low as 30 percent. When managers focus on their people and manage with trust, engagement happens, followed by increased performance and profits.

Harry has taken what he's learned from his previous work and teamed up with John Britt, coauthor of *Who Killed Change?*, and Ed Jent to write the definitive book about achieving excellence in all that you do, *Who Kidnapped Excellence?*

Harry has coauthored six books that have been translated into thirty-five languages and sold well over seven million copies worldwide. His articles on customer service, employee engagement, and workplace culture have been published internationally, and he has been a featured speaker at conferences and corporate meetings in the United States and in places around the world, including Singapore, Bahrain, India, Sri Lanka, Argentina, the Dominican Republic, and Colombia.

Harry lives in San Diego, California, with his wife, and they have two grown children.

Contact Harry

Harry Paul travels the world presenting his ideas and concepts through energized and upbeat keynotes and seminars. He delivers programs based on his mega-best-seller *FISH! A Proven Way to Boost Morale and Improve Results* and other books, such as *Instant Turnaround*, and now *Who Kidnapped Excellence? What Stops Us from Giving and Being Our Best*. For more information on having Harry present to your company or organization, visit his website, www.harrythefishguy.com; e-mail him at Harry@harrythefishguy.com; or call him on his cell phone, (760) 212-8993.

John Britt

John began his career as a registered nurse and worked in a hospital emergency room. It was there that John began to understand that the organization's management and their frontline employees did not share the same perspective. Management seemed interested in discussing staffing,

scheduling, productivity, and efficiencies while the frontline personnel discussed the delivery of patient care and quality for their patients.

After he transitioned to a management position, John began to realize that the leadership, management, and frontline people all ultimately wanted the same thing. They just did not have the same frame of reference, nor did they have the ability to use a common language. This interest in people and the interaction between the various levels of positions led John to go back to get a bachelor's degree in management of human resources and then a master's degree in organizational management.

John eventually began a consulting career in which he had the opportunity to observe and positively influence people in their organizational settings. He became intrigued by the fact that some projects were successful and some were not, and he began a quest to understand this. The quest led him to the topics of change management and change leadership. He began to write down his thoughts and ideas, and it was this path that led to his first book, *Who Killed Change?*, which was coauthored by Ken Blanchard and published in fifteen languages. This book gave John his first major platform to help leadership, management, and frontline personnel to better understand one another's viewpoints.

John was also interested in understanding the impetus for the various levels of customer service he was receiving. Why was it excellent in one establishment and so poor in another? After his father-in-law, whom John was very close to, was killed in a car accident, John became introspective and arrived at his hypothesis: Excellence is inside out. Whether it is customer-service excellence or personal excellence, it begins with a choice and a first step forward. It was this chain of events that led to the writing of *Who Kidnapped Excellence?* John knew that his friends Ed Jent and Harry Paul also had a passion for excellence. Two phone calls later, the collaboration began. John believes that many of the solutions to companies' problems, issues, and challenges can come from their people at the front lines. *Who Kidnapped Excellence?* gives John another platform from which to encourage leadership and management to reach out to their employees.

John is the director of health-care solutions at Kforce, a company that has a history of excellence (see the following section). He speaks nationally and internationally on topics related to organizational behavior. He lives in Louisville, Kentucky, with his wife, Cynthia; three dogs (Dooley, Ellie, and Mollie); and three cats (Dora, Mushu, and Miss Kitty). John's daughter, Katherine, and son, Jonathan, also live in Louisville.

Contact John

John Britt loves speaking with audiences about change, accountability, customer-service excellence, and other organizational behavior topics. He delivers programs around his best-seller *Who Killed Change?*, *Who Pardoned Accountability?*, and now *Who Kidnapped Excellence?* John can be reached at jbritt2468@gmail.com or at (270) 791-2496.

KFORCE

BY JOHN BRITT

Kforce Inc. (NASDAQ: KFRC) is a professional staffing and solutions provider serving the health-care industry since 1998. Kforce's dedicated health-care industry practice offers consulting and project solutions in health information technology, health information management, and revenue life cycle to over five hundred health-care-provider clients nationwide, including 75 percent of the nation's top Honor Roll Hospitals, major health-care insurers, and a large segment of national consulting firms focused on the health-care community ("Best Hospitals 2011–12: The Honor Roll" is an annual list published by *U.S. News & World Report*).

When I first encountered Kforce, I did not know exactly what attracted me to them. Now that I have been associated with them—in fact, become part of the company—I have realized that it is their quest for excellence that drew me in.

Kforce's slogan is "Great People = Great Results," and that is where they put their passion—in recruiting and developing people. Kforce understands that developing their people means promoting competency, allowing for flexibility, facilitating communication, and encouraging ownership.

Ed Jent

Ed graduated from Western Kentucky University (1986) with a bachelor's degree in communication. He also holds a master's degree from Southwestern Baptist Theological Seminary (1988). In addition, he graduated from Walt Disney World's Disney University. It was at Disney that  Ed began to understand what was "behind the curtain" to produce excellence in customer service. He played baseball at Western Kentucky, where he was a cocaptain his senior year. He also traveled with AIA Baseball throughout the Pacific. He has served in Tennessee, Georgia, Texas, and Kentucky as a minister of education for several church organizations. Traveling throughout the world has enabled him to gather a unique cultural perspective on life and people. Some of the best lessons he has learned came from candid conversations with people whom he had nothing in common with.

Ed has committed himself to being a lifelong learner. Change implementation and conflict management are areas he enjoys, in addition to teaching and writing. He is comfortable in front of an audience and loves his work. He is never happier than when he is asked to figure out why something is not working. Counseling and helping others to find their passion is another area he enjoys. Challenging someone to look at something from a different perspective or helping him or her to develop goals inspires Ed.

Working with volunteers in a nonprofit organization offers him an opportunity to be flexible, communicate, instill ownership, develop competency, and be passionate. Leading volunteers for over twenty-five years has been a joy and a privilege. However, leading people who do what they do apart from a salary creates a unique set of opportunities. These five competencies have been the central focus of his work. People excel when they grow in these competencies, and Ed has spent his life helping people to excel.

Family is very important to him, and he enjoys spending time with his wife, Patricia, and his two boys, Hunter and Spencer. Ed lives in Bowling Green, Kentucky.

Contact Ed

Ed Jent would love to speak to your group about excellence! *Who Kidnapped Excellence?* offers a fun way to engage and challenge any audience. What stops us from giving and being our best is a question everyone should answer. His fun, energetic storytelling style will leave you energized and challenged. Ed can be contacted at edjent@gmail.com.

Berrett–Koehler
Publishers

Berrett-Koehler is an independent publisher dedicated to an ambitious mission: *Creating a World That Works for All*.

We believe that to truly create a better world, action is needed at all levels—individual, organizational, and societal. At the individual level, our publications help people align their lives with their values and with their aspirations for a better world. At the organizational level, our publications promote progressive leadership and management practices, socially responsible approaches to business, and humane and effective organizations. At the societal level, our publications advance social and economic justice, shared prosperity, sustainability, and new solutions to national and global issues.

A major theme of our publications is "Opening Up New Space." Berrett-Koehler titles challenge conventional thinking, introduce new ideas, and foster positive change. Their common quest is changing the underlying beliefs, mindsets, institutions, and structures that keep generating the same cycles of problems, no matter who our leaders are or what improvement programs we adopt.

We strive to practice what we preach—to operate our publishing company in line with the ideas in our books. At the core of our approach is stewardship, which we define as a deep sense of responsibility to administer the company for the benefit of all of our "stakeholder" groups: authors, customers, employees, investors, service providers, and the communities and environment around us.

We are grateful to the thousands of readers, authors, and other friends of the company who consider themselves to be part of the "BK Community." We hope that you, too, will join us in our mission.

A BK Business Book

This book is part of our BK Business series. BK Business titles pioneer new and progressive leadership and management practices in all types of public, private, and nonprofit organizations. They promote socially responsible approaches to business, innovative organizational change methods, and more humane and effective organizations.

Berrett–Koehler
Publishers

A community dedicated to creating
a world that works for all

Dear Reader,

Thank you for picking up this book and joining our worldwide community of Berrett-Koehler readers. We share ideas that bring positive change into people's lives, organizations, and society.

To welcome you, we'd like to offer you a free e-book. You can pick from among twelve of our bestselling books by entering the promotional code BKP92E here: http://www.bkconnection.com/welcome.

When you claim your free e-book, we'll also send you a copy of our e-newsletter, the *BK Communiqué*. Although you're free to unsubscribe, there are many benefits to sticking around. In every issue of our newsletter you'll find

- A free e-book
- Tips from famous authors
- Discounts on spotlight titles
- Hilarious insider publishing news
- A chance to win a prize for answering a riddle

Best of all, our readers tell us, "Your newsletter is the only one I actually read." So claim your gift today, and please stay in touch!

Sincerely,

Charlotte Ashlock
Steward of the BK Website

Questions? Comments? Contact me at bkcommunity@bkpub.com.